the Heartbeat *of* IRISH MUSIC

Christy McNamara PHOTOGRAPHS

&

Peter Woods TEXT

ROBERTS RINEHART PUBLISHERS

Published by Roberts Rinehart Publishers

6309 Monarch Park Place

Niwot, Colorado 80503

Distributed to the trade by Publishers Group West

10 9 8 7 6 5 4 3 2 1

First published by The O'Brien Press Ltd.,

20 Victoria Road, Dublin 6, Ireland.

Printed in Canada by Printcrafters

PHOTOGRAPHS: **Front cover**

Joe McNamara of Crusheen. Both Joe and his late brother Paddy played the accordion with the Tulla Céilí Band. Joe is also a singer. He was friendly with Cooley and Tom Power and had a voracious appetite for learning new tunes. Although, as for most of the older musicians in these photos, music took second place to rearing his family, he has never lost his passion for it and has a great memory for songs and tunes. He is a fine storyteller; every incident he talks of he animates, bringing all the characters he has known alive again. Joe is the father of Christy (the photographer for this book).

Back Cover

Claire Keville, from Headford in Galway, is a whistle and concertina player as well as a fine singer. Claire plays in the east Galway style, a style heard in the playing of flute player Paddy Carty and in the playing of Lucy Farr.

Title page

Leah Kelly and her father John. John and his brother James are both noted players; James now lives in America. Their father ran a shop on Capel Street in Dublin; he played the concertina and fiddle, collected music with Seán Ó Riada and gave great encouragement to musicians in the years when it was needed. The Kellys were once regular fixtures at seisiúns around Dublin, particularly in the heyday of music at the Four Seasons pub, playing with the legendary Tommy Potts. The Crehans are all members of Junior Crehan's extended family.

Contents

Acknowledgments iv

Prologue v

PART ONE—from the twenties to the fifties

Last Night's Fun 1

Music From a Table 21

The Wheels of the World 25

My Love Is In America 39

The Brown Coffin 47

The Camden Reel 57

PART TWO—from the fifties to the seventies

Banish Misfortune 77

Beating Snow Off a Rope 89

PART THREE—the eighties and the nineties

Piseogs 101

The Roaring Twenties 111

Reels at the End of the World 127

PART FOUR—between the generations

The Night Before the Fleadh 143

Acknowledgments

CHRISTY: Thanks to my parents, Joe and Biddy, for introducing me to the music, and to my brothers and sisters, my grandmother, Molly, and all of my family for their help and encouragement, and to all the musicians that I've got to know over the years.

To Adrian Ensor (London), for his expertise in the dark room, his patience and his continuing support—another mission, but not an impossible one; Lawrence Dunmore for design advice on exhibitions; Liam MacNamara; Jim Robson; George Kavanagh; Gareth McCarthy; Steve Wilson (Photolab Techniques); Sara Lloyd (Ilford UK); Julie Brown (MAP, London); Rob Willis (Process Supplies, London); Harry Collins and Susie Keane (Nikon UK); Jonathan Tops (Fuji UK); Eddie Shanahan (Dublin); Primary Colour (Dublin); Augostinho Pedrosa (Portugal); Mike Mulcair (Ennis); Photo World (Ennis).

PETER: All the musicians represented in this book; all those stories subsumed; all those late nights in the Fiddler's and elsewhere, and for the music that can't be ended; Tim O'Grady; my sister, Déirdre, and the rest of my family—the Woods—at their most extended—for the story had to start somewhere. But mostly thanks are due to my wife, Eileen, and to my very wonderful daughter, Sorchadh, for suffering all of this.

TOGETHER: Ollie Frowley from Kilkee for the introduction; Íde ní Laoghaire, our editor; Vincent DeVeau and the bank manager.

Katherine and Barbara O'Grady, twin sisters from Kilnaboy on the Burren, County Clare.

Prologue

There were localities and there were families that were always involved in the music. Their fathers before them played and it was handed down and their houses were given free to anyone who'd play music or dance a set. There was a concertina in every house. You could buy a concertina for five bob or seven-and-six then, or a three-stop melodion for a pound. There was an old woman who lived near the foot of that hill there, Missus Cuneen, she was a good concertina player. Jim McEnerney, "Jim The Bull," was a good

DEDICATION
*Ciarán agus Paul
ar dheis Dé go
raibh a
n-anamacha
uaisle dílse*

concertina player. Down there Pet Flanagan's father Mick Flanagan, "The Jig," he was a good concertina player, and his father before him was a noted fiddler—he went by the name "The Giant Flanagan." Delia Littleton was a good concertina player too; but her sisters bought a fiddle, span new, rigged out in a case—four pound was a lot of money then but they were good players; they had a lot of music.

JOE MCNAMARA

the Heartbeat of IRISH MUSIC

PART ONE
from the twenties to the fifties

Bridie Callinan and Kathleen O'Loughlin dancing a set in Bridie's kitchen in Ruan, the way it used to be done, in a house noted for the clattering of dancers' feet.

Last Night's Fun

Karen Ryan on her wedding day in Feakle, County Clare.

*T*here was music before me and after me—on both sides of my family they could play. There was music in nearly every house where we came from, up in the humps and hollows, wet, bad land, all bog and lake. Music was all people had as a diversion from their everyday lives; music and hurling and maybe a hand of cards. But in the music you didn't rely on anyone else—it was within you and you could take it with you wherever you went in life. Good musicians were remembered even if they'd emigrated; people spoke of the piper Garret Barry, who was long dead in the Poor House in Ennistymon, as if he were still wandering the roads. The music was always there.

The night I was born there were forty-three swans on the lake you could see from our house, a pure sign of storm, and I was born of a stormy night into stormy times. The year was 1919 and it was round the time that a gang of men, up in Soloheadbeg in Tipperary, ambushed an RIC dynamite convoy and started the country's War of Independence.

By the time I was old enough to question it, most of those who'd taken part, from round our

way, were in England or America, like my father's brother Ownie. My mother and her people would have no part in it; she used to joke about my father's family out with guns. But my father had carried on as if nothing out of the way was happening. One day he was in the town and the Black and Tans took him for his brother. They marched him backwards, two miles out the road, in front of a Crossley Tender; he said they'd all been drinking. He thought they were going to kill him. They stood him up against a wall and blindfolded him. He could hear someone's hand scrabbling against a holster flap, and a voice said in his ear: "When they shoot stand up. In the trenches a man who crouched down took it in the belly. Better in the legs." He heard the impact of a bullet on both sides of his head and then a burning sensation in his legs and he fell over on the road. He lay there. The Black and Tans

Gerdy Commane from Ballyknock, near Kilmona, a fine concertina player in the west Clare style. Clare more than any other county is associated with the concertina. The usual explanation for this is that sailors brought it ashore in the ports in the last century. And concertinas were cheap. Gerdy, and most musicians of his age, learned to play the Anglo-German concertina—this is single-action, sounding the same note whether pushed or drawn. Junior Crehan tells of the arrival of the first English concertina in Miltown Malbay. An Englishman was endeavoring to interest the customers in a bar in its qualities, but no one wanted to buy it and the man left. A Guard, stationed in the town, came in and wanted to know what the stranger was after. When he heard, "he took off out the road after him and bought it from him," as Junior says. The double-action concertina became the standard in Clare and wherever else it was played, and musicians like Gerdy adapted it to their own style of playing.

got back into their Tender and left him for dead, all but the man who had told him not to crouch over. All he ever had from it was a bad memory and a bit of a limp.

My father married in his middle forties—in those days that was not unusual, for a man at any rate. He had no time for music although he could play himself. I remember hearing him once, his reedy breath hardly able to fill the flute. His whole life was a struggle with bad land to feed us. He gave up taking any pleasure in tunes. But he could find water with a sally rod; it was a gift I never inher-ited. I can remember the one time I tried it. We were standing in our kitchen, there was a spring directly beneath us and I was holding the rod. I could feel nothing. He took hold of my two wrists and a force surged through me—it was like electricity travelling beneath my skin in bumps, up my arms. It was a feeling I only ever had

Last
Night's
Fun

3

one other time in my life and that was playing music.

We lived up in the lea of a hill in a place called Altandown. The climb from the town up there was four miles. The townspeople considered it the back of beyond. You'd hear them of a fair day in the town saying: "Whose is that young fella?" "He's one of the Ruanes from out the back of the hill." It was like living at sea up there, each hill piling up like a wave, so that when you crested one, there was always another one after it and another one, until you came to our townland and it flattened out to where the church was. The church was built before the Famine in the 1840s. Behind it was our house and the last hill, a lone bush on top of it. Beyond that the land began to run downhill again, four miles in the other direction.

Altandown: even the word itself had a kind of music for me. Altandown itself was called after the fort at the top of the hill—it meant "the roof of the world," and you could see a great distance from there, the lake glinting before you, farther than most people would have travelled in those times.

I would like to be able to let on that I came from a house cluttered with pictures of paunchy men and ample-breasted women—my forebears—but I didn't. The world I lived in was fixed by its existence—we were there, on twenty-eight acres of bad land. That was enough. In those times people didn't worry too much about how they came to be in a place. There wasn't much to our house. We had one big room that was a kitchen and a kind of living room. Above it was a loft where myself and my brother slept and where things were stored until they were forgotten about. Behind that there was the single bedroom where my mother and father slept.

It is my mother I can blame for the music. She was a McMahon and they were noted musicians, from one generation to the next. They had a fair parcel of land, and at one time had lime kilns and flax on the go as well. By my mother's time this had all gone. She was the youngest of them. Her elder brother sold the land and went to America for reasons nobody knew, although people talked about it; it was a source of wonderment that he walked out on good land. People still talked about him as if he were living locally. Because I never knew him—he was long gone before my time—it was hard for me to think of him alive, but think of him I did; his music had left a powerful impression. It was said he had a world of tunes. We never heard anything from him but rumors and when I asked my mother about him she seemed reluctant to talk. I'd say there was bad feeling involved—my mother got no dowry when she was married. That was unusual in those times when even a girl entering a convent would have brought money with her. The only thing she would ever say was that we had his fire if he ever came back.

In those times if someone went to America and a house was emptied out, the neighbors would take a blazing sod of turf from that hearth and place it in their own—in that way the fire was kept alive for the people if they came back. You'd hear of houses that had three or four fires in them, and that's what people would mean. The McMahons' old place was at the other side of the hill, at the back of Altandown. If bad land had to end and good land start somewhere, then that was where it happened: Lisnamac. The house was long neglected and tumbling in on itself when I was growing up. To get there you had to go up the old, cobbled, Famine road that started at the church. The road meandered to an end in the middle of a field, and from there you took the pad. The pad had been worn into the ground by hundreds of journeys. It would take you through the trees and up to the house.

It was unusual in the country to come across trees that had been deliberately planted, yet never cut down for timber. It was as if the man who bought the land from McMahon had forgotten he owned it. Coniferous trees were, in themselves, a sign of wealth. You'd see them outside the houses of Protestant people, dotted through the country. In the open, windswept land, on the hills of Altandown and Lisnamac, they stood out. Anyone who planted trees was drawing a line, saying, "This is my property." With the ruined house, they gave the place a kind of ghostly air.

It was said that Lisnamac townland was cursed, that you'd never hear a bird singing there. I used to go up and sit in the trees and just listen to the wind rustling through them. Even the smell of coniferous trees has, for me, a rhythm of its own, a strangeness that's almost sacred, like frankincense burning in an empty church. After a while it would grow so still, and without the sounds of birds, I'd begin to think of all the generations that had passed along that path and of my uncle returning from his revels, the fiddle wrapped under his arm, whistling a tune. It was a place I could never go to but be sensible of music.

My mother was a fine musician. I used to hear the old people talking about her and in that way I knew she was good. In those days a woman who got married would have to give up playing to rear her family—it was part of the bargain. Our house, like most houses at that time, had a concertina in the hob, by the fire. She could play the concertina and the whistle, and whenever she went out I'd sneak the concertina down and try to make shapes from it. Music was like that for me then, just color and shape. I used to think that if you played loud enough it would fill the room to bursting—you'd be as well leaving a window open; or maybe it seeped out under the door, like a grey mist across the countryside.

When she found me she'd kill me. But I used to pester her, following her round her jobs, until she showed me the fingering on the whistle. I picked up a few simple tunes from her that way. Then she let me try the concertina. She did it as much to keep me quiet as anything else, at least at first. Then she saw that I was serious about it and she encouraged me in any way she could. She used to come between me and my father and argue for me being let play in my time off.

When I think of her now she's always lilting a jig or a reel. Try as I might I can only get snatches of those tunes. She had tunes no one else had. She must have come up with them herself, but, because she died young, I never got the music I should have from her. By the time I'd found my own way in music, the McMahons were dead for me, except for the stories about them that lived on.

The McMahons were said to have been cursed; it was said that the day would come when none of them would live in Lisnamac. Most people didn't pass any remarks on these curses and those who did talked about them in low voices. People were like that. If someone died belonging to you they'd shake your hand and say sorry for your trouble and they'd milk your cows for you and help in any way they could; if something ailed you they'd tell you about someone who was worse off than you were. They were like that about curses

too, *piseogs* they called them, and then they'd say that curses returned to roost at home; if they did come to pass they'd talk about them in low voices.

There was one fiddle player who was one of those cursed McMahons, my mother's people. He was the last of those McMahons. He was a great man for learning tunes. He'd travel far and near in search of a new tune. Older musicians liked him because he always paid his dues, mentioning where he'd learned a tune or whose setting he was playing. He had the name of a practical joker; once he scared a man returning from a card-school in the early hours by playing his fiddle in a grave-yard, him perched above on a headstone. Well, that man's hair turned grey with the shock. McMahon had a fair parcel of land which he farmed in the summer and let lie fallow in the winter months—selling his cattle off, he'd take to the roads with his fiddle under his arm.

This McMahon had a lot of cures which had been in the family. They said you'd see him betimes abroad in the fields picking plants to make infusions. It was on one of these occasions, one springtime, he was searching through a clump of nettles for the young tender shoots and the rarer plants that grew in their shelter, when something came over him. A mist like the mists that gather in the hollows of fields of a fine summer morning rose about him and he felt overcome by hunger and weakness. He was afflicted, rooted to the ground. There was a rushing sound in his ears like the wind sawing through empty trees. The air was heavy and difficult to breathe and that set his heart galloping. He could see people about him, rooting around, scouring the earth. People in their hundreds sinking into the ground, eating grass and dying in the ditches, fading away before him. It was like he was at the bottom of a drain, the glar tugging him down into it, hampering every step he took. The smell of it rising about him, a smell that filled him with yearning and a terrible hunger and great pain. The sound of the wind became the cries of women keening and through that there came music. It was like no music he'd ever heard before, like the torrent that collapsed the walls of a graveyard sweeping the bodies of the dead back out among the living, like graveyards of sorrow, like rotting ships taking to sea sinking beneath the weight of their passengers, people fleeing from death to uncertainty. It closed in upon him like the unearthly boom of geese flying low over water, lost in a November mist, the sky pressing down on them. And then it all subsided and he found himself on his knees in a clump of nettles in his own field, heaving dryly on an empty stomach.

McMahon returned to his own house that day and lay on his bed as if he were grieving for someone he'd never known. He neglected his land altogether after that, renting it out as conacre to big farmers who grazed it clean, took their use out of it and let it run to rushes. He could be seen in that field at all hours, bent close to the ground. When he turned to play music afterwards he'd play a reel or two as if to warm up and then he'd drift off, bowing a few solitary notes or a phrase of an air no one had ever heard before. More often than not he'd turn the same phrase again and again or begin in mid-phrase with nothing to follow it. He'd lay his head on its side along the fiddle, listening, as if the fiddle might have, in its hidden recesses, an answer. He'd rephrase and rephrase, but the tune would not come.

There's a story told about another fiddle-player, by the name of Paddy Daly, who had the gift of dreaming music which he could then play. All went well until one night he dreamt the best music he'd ever heard and dreamt it happened at his own funeral. There he was, laid out in his coffin, the fiddle across his chest, his fingers with death's grip on the bow and the music in full spate about him. Each of his friends, musicians he'd known who were dead and gone and others who were still of this earth, flute, concertina and melodion players, pipers and whistlers, as well as men he knew who hadn't a notion of music, and each and every one of them playing a fiddle. One after another they improvised on a jig; as one would cease to play another would take it up, turning it again in a new direction, adding new parts to it, until it seemed it would never cease—it grew like

Mary Ellen Reidy from Ennistymon. Mary Ellen is one of the few women musicians of her generation still playing music. It was in the 'sixties that music first began to be played widely in pubs in Ireland— for older musicians this was unknown; music was something they often played just for their own enjoyment —it was a private thing—or for that of a few friends.

Junior Crehan from Bonabilla, near The Crosses of Annagh, County Clare. Junior learned his music from Scully Casey, father of Bobby Casey, a legendary player whose compositions are still played. Like most of the older musicians in these photos, Junior lived through times when the future of the music looked bleak. A great storyteller, he talks of those days and of the demise of the house dances. He also composes music.

an old steam threshing mill, turned in on itself, that couldn't stop. He felt himself come through the door into the room where the wake was being held. "What do you call that tune?" he asked an old acquaintance of his. The man turned to him and said, without recognizing him, "It's called "Paddy Daly's Dream." He found himself back in the coffin and struggle as he might he couldn't rise from it.

After that he dreamt many strange things. He dreamt that unbeknownst to him he'd ignored and then tried to kill an uncle of his in a place he'd never been in before. He dreamt the results of different sports meetings. But whatever he dreamt, none of it bore any resemblance to music again. Music had moved beyond his scope; it all sounded to him like the sounds rooks make in their high, bare nests as they convoke in April. Try as he might afterwards he couldn't catch a single phrase of that jig, no more than he could rise from his own coffin in his dream. In the end he was so far gone he killed himself thinking that that was the only way he'd know the music played at his own wake.

Well, McMahon knew this story and it frightened him. He went to see the priest about it and the priest told him to be about his own trans-

Ennistymon, County Clare.

actions, not to meddle in things he knew nothing of. He said the divil had a hand in it and that the most powerful music of all was silence. There were reasons why there was no music from Famine times and then the priest wondered aloud at God's ways that so often gave the best voices to sinners.

Eventually McMahon sold up and went to America as if the clanking machinery and the great canyons between the tall buildings of that country might somehow diminish the music that haunted him. Going to America then was like a contract with the divil. It wasn't like England, a place you were in on sufferance, for some a purgatory and then a limbo with no remission. With America, you couldn't renege or come back, although people always held out hope. But when they took the last glowing ember from his hearth to plant in their own, his neighbors whispered among themselves that things had run their course and the curse had been fulfilled. The night before he left they had an American wake and he got violently ill and dreamt that when he turned to play music curdled milk flowed from the soundpost of his fiddle.

At first in America he drifted from one place to another as the work took him. He was an engineer on the railways and then he worked on the skyscrapers, erecting steel. But whatever he did the notes of that tune were there to haunt him. They were there when he rode the high girders, zinging about the suspension cables, and there in the stench of burning human flesh that never left his nostrils when he worked as a fireman in Philadelphia, and there the time he lifted a human body, caught above a boiling factory vat, when the steamed flesh fell away in his hands leaving him cradling a skeleton.

There's them that said he never played a tune after and others who said he was seen playing in shebeens and speakeasies and that his music had taken on a fierce lonesomeness, that it was better for listening to than for dancing to.

But there was one photo taken of him, one of the first pictures taken of Irish musicians in the New World and the men in it look as if they are transfixed by the awesomeness of it—got up in their Sunday best, posing formally as if staring down the twin barrels of a shotgun. Their names, townlands and counties are inscribed beneath them. For some reason the band in the photograph was said to have belonged to a Jack Coen from over in east Galway. But when people went to check up on this Coen in the townland from where he was said to have come there was no record of such a man. It transpired that the Coen in question was a Cohen, an eastern European musician who sat in with the band in order to earn a few dollars. This was not uncommon at that time. The real band leader was a Jack Mulalley from Mayo.

Mulalley's daughter in Philadelphia

unearthed an old wax cylinder recording he had made at the World's Fair in Chicago in 1893. She said he used to talk of having gone there with a fiddle player named McMahon to hear Patsy Touhey, the legendary piper. Touhey had made the first wax cylinder recording and had convinced Mulalley and McMahon to join him. She said that her father had talked about McMahon recording a strange air; he said his fiddling was like voltage running in chains across the distant tops of the skyscrapers in a storm. She said her father had the wax cylinder and used to play it, but that it—like so much else of the figure, with the fiddle cradled against him, staring out from sepia as if he had no purchase on this earth—had either been lost or destroyed. Even in the sepia his image seems to have faded faster than that of the other musicians. Unlike them it appears as if there's more choking him than the high collar and stud on his shirt, as if he were already fading.

Maybe McMahon knew more than the rest of us; they say that the man born to be hung cannot be drowned. At any rate, little was heard of him. There's no record surviving, and one way or another his music was lost. There's musicians that are driven to take the step that isn't there, and even though they know that themselves, they struggle to play the music they hear in their heads. They might think they're going mad because they can't explain it to anybody—we all have stories we can

never tell and we all tread lightly on this earth. If you wanted a fiddle you could have one made locally. Shop-bought fiddles were expensive and rare. You had families like the Dinans over in Maghera who made instruments. They made carts mostly, and the fiddles were a sideline. They made the old-style Russian fiddle, the triangular one. The wood came from everywhere—from the shafts of carts and the tines of traps, from elder and sycamore, imported lancewood and greenheart that they used for fishing-rods—wood from all over the world. There was one fiddle I still remember in a house down the road from us and you could see that the soundpost was made from an old school-desk. They were simple enough instruments and nowadays they have better gear for making fiddles, but many's the tune was learned and many's the fine musician started out on the Russian fiddle.

One day, when they were all out, I was rummaging through the stuff they had stored in the loft where we slept—a cardboard suitcase, old papers and photos of my mother's people; sad things, mostly, like you'd find in an empty house, when I came across the fiddle. It was wrapped in a piece of old sacking, a bow alongside it. It wasn't a good fiddle, but I couldn't believe my luck. It might have belonged to my uncle, I never found out—it was like it wasn't supposed to be there. I could see the maker's stamp on it. There were

Joe McNamara of Crusheen. Both Joe and his late brother Paddy played the accordion with the Tulla Céilí Band. Joe is also a singer. He was friendly with Cooley and Tom Power and had a voracious appetite for learning new tunes. Although, as for most of the older musicians in these photos, music took second place to rearing his family, he has never lost his passion for it and has a great memory for songs and tunes. He is a fine storyteller; every incident he talks of he animates, bringing all the characters he has known alive again. Joe is the father of Christy (the photographer for this book).

Last
Night's
Fun

only two strings, but I wound them up and down until I got a tune from it. That tune was "The Wearing of the Green." I'm sure now it must have sounded bad, but to my childish ears it was a miracle and nothing would do but I'd get the other two strings.

People who didn't like music, who it was just noise to, would tell you music would make you lazy. If that was true then I started out in the right way. From an early age I'd run up into the fields with the whistle. They said I used to imitate the sounds of the birds. When the weather was bad I'd plant myself in a cupboard, a blanket pulled down over the door to deaden the sound, and play away to my heart's content. Nothing would deflect me from the music. When I did get the strings I put them on wrong, but I still got music from that fiddle, between twisting up and twisting down, getting the right note and the right finger, my brother shouting, "Who's drowning the cat?" The determin-ation I had—I had three or four tunes before I'd finished. Between the whistle and the concertina I had it in the hands. Then I had it in the head.

There was an old man up the road from us and it was him who made a fiddler of me. Even now I still think of him as an old man, though I suppose he must have been young enough then. He wasn't a man who went out much and it was by accident I first heard him playing, at a wedding.

I was chasing some of the other children through the kitchen where the dancing was going on, when his notes caught me and I stopped to listen. From that day I followed him everywhere. That was in 1930, just before my father died.

My father went out to milk the cows one evening. I was inside with my brother Tom and my mother when we heard the cows bawling. We'd passed no remarks on the length of time he was out. He was a busy man and was hardly in the house for anything other than food and sleep. I went out to the shed and found him lying on his back. Tom ran across the fields to the neighbors' houses and Mick Talty and old Joe Considine came over and carried him into the house on a door. One week I was out playing with a hurling stick, letting on it was a gun, and the next week I knew, without being told, that I could never do that again. After that I was a man, although I didn't know what that meant. I was the oldest.

My mother started to live in a house full of ghosts—she was back up in the McMahons of her youth, when they had serving girls in the house and men to help with the land and kilns. Me and Tom were drifting about of our own free will. Apart from scouring a living from the fields I could do what I wanted. I was finished at school and whatever spare time I had I spent up at that old man's house.

I'd go and stand outside and look in at him

going about his business. At first he took me for a bit simple, as if my father's death had deranged me. But he was sympathetic to me and made a bit of a joke of me. He'd offer me a sip from the mug of porter he might have. But I wouldn't leave him alone. The odd time he showed up to play at a house, I'd be there.

I was in awe of him and I never spoke to him yet. I used to lie awake at night wondering how he kept so much music in his head. I never let on I had the fiddle myself. Then, one day, he handed his fiddle to me. I can still see the laughter in his eyes change as I scratched out "The Britches." "I thought," he says, "all the music stopped when your uncle left the country." I told him I was going to be better than my uncle ever was. "Then you'll be better than I ever will," he said. I asked him to teach me. He wasn't on for it. There were plenty of travelling music teachers around the country, plenty of men who needed the few pence going for teaching. But it was his sound I wanted to imitate. Still, he showed me how to string the fiddle right, showed me the odd note and how a certain tune was turned. In the heel of the hunt he gave in and asked me up to his house. He had no family, that man, and I think in the end he was afraid of the music dying with him.

He had lovely soft melody and great volume to his playing. The only way he'd play was sitting down at the fire. Every night I went to him I'd get one or maybe two tunes from him. I spent all my free time with him. If I had a wrong note he'd correct me. He gave me great encouragement. He would stand with his back to me, over at the window looking out. I'd stand at the fire, with the fiddle under my chin. Sometimes I'd think he wasn't listening, but he was always listening, whistling along with me.

"By God," he'd say, "that should be an up-bow not a down-bow. You're not hearing the music in your head. You have to hear it in your head." He'd take the fiddle off me and essay the tune again and when he'd finished, with the sunlight streaming in the window, you could feel the notes hanging in the air. It was like looking into a loft as they shook out oats, watching the chaff floating down. He had the gift of music, that man.

He told me I had talent but I needed to take my time. He said no matter how much I loved the music there was no living in it, or what few bob you might glean from teaching lessons wouldn't feed you. He told me to mind the land, that was what would feed us. But music, he said, never left you. I was in too much of a hurry. It took time, he told me. If I mastered the basics, got the fingering and tempo right the rest would follow easily. He taught me to think of how the music worked, how the tunes had secret joins—their form—and eventually how to embellish them. He made me think of the start of each tune as a question and the turn of the tune as the answer; an assertion and a response. In the great tunes the responses just burst out of you. They were the times when the listeners would roar and yelp encouragement, the dancers would batter the floor, the times when you could loosen things in people that they didn't know were there. You couldn't hurry that, but it was worth waiting for.

The turn in the tune was like an elbow in your arm, he said, if it was working right so was everything else. Later I thought of the turn as a woman you fought to possess; sometimes she moved away from you.

But what he did most for me was to show me how to hold the music in my head. It was like imagining it into being. A tune could be attached to a story or, if I liked, I might take a roundabout route to his house and go over the twists and turns of the tune in my head as I walked, attaching notes to ditches and trees and to the twists in the road, hanging notes on bushes, gaps and gates. Wherever I went in the years after I could never think of the roads around home without a part of a tune coming to me, or start to play any tune without thinking of those roads and ditches. He told me stories of musicians I'd never heard anyone else even name, men and women that were long dead in the bad times past. He told me the country used to be alive with pipers, that his own people and those of my father had piped and that was where his music really came from. He told me of

musicians who had been given tunes by the fairies, but, he said, he himself had never known that to happen. Those stories were just ways of explaining other things that men got it hard to talk about. He had a way of making the past inhabit the present, of increasing the importance of every tune, of every note.

He gave me a grasp of things I would have lacked otherwise. I learned to place the music at the center of my life in such a way that people wouldn't even know it was there. The old man's swinging style became mine. He could see clearly what was false. When I'd play a sad note he'd tell me that it didn't belong to me, it was copied and I was too young to feel those notes, but then, one day, I heard him tell my mother that I was born with those sad notes in me, and I wondered. I wondered because all I thought I was doing was copying him. Even when he was whistling a tune he seemed to dwell on certain notes and they took on a lonesomeness because of that. What he had in the lyrical way he played would be lost when he played with other musicians—you had to hear him on his own. I didn't know you could be born with the lonesome music in you. I knew there was sad music and happy music. I knew that before I learned to play at all, it was just that that man could play the two sorts of music at the one time. He bewildered me.

He gave me a tune one time that he said had

been written by a piper the first time he'd seen the sea. But the piper didn't see the sea, he felt it—his eyes, the old man said, were as useful to him as those that grow in the damp dark are to a spud. He said that for men who'd seen the sea, the lake you could see from our house was just a puddle. That was why so few that left ever came back. The thing about that piper was, he said, that through the force of his imagination he could make people see the red sun going down, coloring the water and the sand.

He had his own way of thinking about everything. The music was never enough for him. He was always wondering about the other things that went to make it up—the sound of the sea and the names of the tunes. In what bog were those geese and who was the boy in the gap? These, too, became the things I pondered, scratching my head and scratching out tunes, agonizing over problems that wouldn't bother a man in his right mind.

For musicians weren't highly thought of then. If music was religion to some of us it was the divil to others. When I was at school and they went on about original sin, I used to think it was the music they meant, because that was the way my father saw it; it was something that took hold of you, interfering with work and the likes, and once it took hold of you there was no going back.

The old man had a story he used to tell of a time he was coming back from a wedding. "It was at night we'd go out mostly," he said. "Anyhow, I was coming back in the bright of the morning. When I came into my own way down here I met a man. He was looking for a cow that had gone rambling.

"Where were you till this hour?"

"I was at a wedding."

"And you stayed till this hour?"

"We did," says I. Now, that man wouldn't spend a shilling. "We stayed till the porter was drank and then we came home."

"O God in heavens," says he, "what have you in that box?"

"Young cats," says I. I was letting the odd stagger and he had great pity for me. He could see that I was going wrong. But just then didn't a string go.

"Well," says he, "if you don't get rid of them cats you'll not live much longer."

"Well, that man is gone now and there isn't a word about him or his kind, and I'm still here, still playing. His like were never any use to anyone."

Whatever that old man did, what he taught me would never leave me. No matter how bad things got, the music was always there.

The Dinan family of Maghera. Michael is playing while his mother, 102 years old when the picture was taken, listens in the opposite corner. Michael has made many fiddles, both triangular and standard, and he has also made a three-quarter viola. Though the Dinans are farmers, his father before him made instruments. They also made carts and, as Michael says himself, "I made every wheel that ever turned."

Michael is a great lover of the music of Eddie Reavey, the Cavan fiddle player who emigrated to America at an early age. Reavey was a composer with a phenomenal output of tunes, and Michael taught himself to read music so he could learn them from sheet music, as recordings of Reavey were hard to come by. Michael's music came down from his mother who plays the concertina.

Music From a Table

The invention of the gramophone and its arrival in Ireland changed the music forever. Its coming was like magic and the old people recalled ancient prophecies that the news would come down the chimney and music from a table. The Victrolas arrived from America and for a family to have one meant that they hadn't been forgotten by those who had left. In those times people couldn't easily come back and the few dollars they sent were used to send someone else out or appeared in the form of something useful like a better roof on a house. Those dollars were often called "money for slates," the slate that replaced the thatch.

We thought the streets of America were truly paved with gold, or with dollars at least, and it was only in later years, when I'd gone away from home myself, that I realized how hard-earned that money was. To own a suit sent back from the States was a big thing then. You'd notice the men that had family in America outside Mass of a Sunday, all got up in those blue suits, the trousers with turn-ups, like the Americans we would later see in gangster films. Indeed, it would be easier to count them that hadn't family there, so plentiful were those blue suits.

The Victrola, though, was purely for pleasure. It meant a lot to people that America, the one country we all looked up to, put enough value on our music to record it. People who had put no value on it themselves began to listen, and that in turn gave some musicians a sense of their own importance. The fact that the most popular records were by the Sligomen Michael Coleman and James Morrison meant that, for many people, their music was considered the best. After all, if the Americans thought so . . .

In the 1920s, it was Coleman's tunes like "Bonnie Kate" and "Lord Gordon's" and his settings of tunes that began to be heard all over the country. Those tunes and settings are still played the same today and there are still those—younger musicians among them—who believe that that was the time when the music was at its height. To have had a fiddle in New York in the 1920s was the best that could have happened to you.

They sent the 78s over as they got them—they were often the only way there was of learning a new tune. You'd slow it down to catch the note. There was a woman across the fields from us and she had a great stack of 78s, of Coleman and Morrison. I used to get the loan of them off her. She'd give me two every Sunday night going home, warning me not to break them—they were very delicate. The journey was all cross-country then you know, and no priest ever held the host with the reverence I did those old recordings, crossing the fields in the dark, snatches of the latest tune running through my head, wondering about the fingering and, all the while, my feet sure of their own path home.

I'd take the gramophone down into the room on my own, or wait till they were all out and nobody could tell me to stop, teasing out the notes until I turned the tune. Every week I'd have two new tunes. My old teacher didn't have a gramophone, and I used to go up and play the tunes to him; what it took me a week to master he could turn in half an hour. He was awful quick to pick up a tune. He was like a bone-setter reaching in to find what was important and knitting it all together. It was never just the notes with him—it was the notes between the notes. I remember once playing "The Old Grey Goose" for him, there's six or seven parts to it. "O Lord," he says, "there's fistfuls of music in that jig. Fistfuls."

What you'd want from those tunes would be the style. A good enough player could take Coleman's style and adapt it to his own, adding a bit here or taking away a bit there. A good player would never copy directly. A great player had his own style. But even to copy Coleman you had to be a handy enough player, to get all the flourishes he had in "Bonnie Kate." Listening to his playing of a tune you already knew would leave you wondering why you couldn't have thought of those flourishes yourself.

But for all the speed in that music it felt distant

and far away as if it was echoing back to you from a far-off room. Maybe that has got to do with Coleman himself and the way he ended up, for all his fame, frozen stiff on a park bench. And you would think of the dollars and the Victrolas and of all those who sent them and never got to come back. I think of myself below in that room, cranking that handle like the handle on the old-fashioned telephone, having a musical conversation with people so far away. The spirit of Coleman in everything. Going to bed after a night playing with him, imitating him. The time I heard "The Sailor's Bonnet," coming after "The Tarbolton" and "The Longford Collector," which was also called "The Longford Beggarwoman." I would have stood to my neck in icy water listening to that man; he put the hairs standing on me. Even today I can still remember the feeling I had waiting for the needle to descend on one of those old 78s for the first time. The kind of fuzzy background sound they often had, the piano player often out of sympathy with the music. It was always, for me at any rate, very wistful music, like ghost music nearly, like when I first heard "The Grey Goose" coming back to us from America.

Maybe the music is like everything else and it follows its own fashion. A musician that was well known thirty years ago is nearly unknown now. Some people don't like to play certain tunes—"The Bucks of Oranmore," for example.

They think they've been played to death; but a good tune is always a good tune. Think of Joe Cooley's "Wise Maid." Think of the life and the drive and the fire in "The Bucks." Martin Hayes still plays "The Britches." That's an old tune, played in different settings all over the country. It's a simple tune and his version of it follows Joe Bane, the whistle player from Feakle. When Bane played it in a session it was like a lull in a conversation, a breathing space. He learned it from Paddy Canny's father, Martin's uncle. Listening to Martin play it, it's like music from a seance—it goes way back, that tune.

Maybe there are no new tunes. Maybe we're just remembering the thousands of old tunes we've forgotten. Like old Missus Dinan, over 105 years of age and dreaming a hornpipe every night until eventually she played it—a tune like that dreamt out of the air—a dream tune. Maybe the music all those musicians played in America and England and before they went is still there waiting for someone to dream it back, just waiting for someone to put a form on it.

The Wheels of the World

A seisiún in Queally's Pub, Miltown Malbay, County Clare.

For some people, like my brother Tom, what happened beyond us was always more real than what happened at home. Tom never had the drive to play music that I had. But he could play. He learned because he wanted to be involved in what happened around the music—the craic, as we called it—and the few tunes were his entrance fee to that. He learned the fingering on a toy flute he got one Christmas—there was no flute in our house so he had to buy one. He saved for it in pennies. Twelve-and-six was an awful lot of pennies. The man he bought it from went to America. One night, myself and Tom were playing at a sports dance in a school and a man came up to the stage. "That's my old flute," he said. "I'd know that tone anywhere." Well, he joined us for a few tunes and him and Tom got talking. When we were making our way home that night Tom turned to me and said, "That's it. My mind's made up. I'm going to America." And that was it; he was gone within a month.

The gramophone was one of the first signs, though we didn't know it then, that the world was getting to be a smaller place. One of the great tunes

Micho Russell. Micho was one of the great characters of the music world. The day this photo was taken he was just back from playing at a big festival in Norway; he was playing "Miss Monaghan," and talking of the shipwreck the crowbar behind him had come from, of the importance of having names for tunes, of the Aran islands beyond him, and of the Liscannor flagstones his brother Pakie had laid on the kitchen floor. Sadly, Micho was killed in a car crash shortly afterwards. There are many recordings of him, notably the one he made with Pakie and his other brother Gussie: "The Russell Family of Doolin, County Clare."

I learned was "The Wheels of the World." I got it from the playing of James Morrison. Just the name of it alone seemed to me to stand for everything that was outside of us. And in Altandown we had been living a life that was disconnected from what was real and happening elsewhere. That, of course, wasn't true. We were always prey to what happened in other places. Two of my mother's brothers enlisted and died in the Great War. We'd got the potatoes, and the blight that came on them, from the New World. What happened beyond us would always eventually wash up at our door.

One of the first signs of the Depression in America was the end of the 78s. There was less money for diversion, and music was the first thing to suffer. There were no gramophone records anymore and few being recorded. We were again starved for new tunes. At the best of times the only music that would be about would be the same few tunes that had been played over and over down the years, tunes like "Last Night's Fun" and "The Bag of Spuds." You'd rely for learning on the travelling musicians and on the men that might travel seven miles one direction and you another seven to meet at a fair or a wake or some social gathering. Those that had new tunes would often be reluctant to part with them, but they came in by degrees.

In later years when the box player Joe Cooley was about these parts he was a notorious traveller. He was as likely to be in this house here as he was

to be above with Máirtín Byrnes in Castlefinnerty or with Tony Reddon, a Galwayman who played in goals for the Tipperary hurlers, down in Tipperary. Cooley would travel anywhere for a night's music or sport. He might have engagements to play with two different bands of the one night.

Cooley's accordion playing made a great impression on all those who heard him. He had great energy and style. Everything for him was wrapped up in emotion. There was at the time, and there have been since, technically better players, faster players, players who know their way round the box better than Joe did, but it was always about Joe that you'd find the crowd gathered, looking at him, watching him drive his whole body behind his box. You could be standing at the back of a place when Cooley came to play, the place emptied out into the corners, but when he strapped on the box and launched into a tune the crowds would start towards him, even if they didn't know who he was. He inspired people. Oh, they'd say, can't he make it talk.

I met another man from Tipperary in London once. He used to work with Cooley on the railways. He was a bit of a box player himself but hadn't played since he'd left home. Cooley got him at it again and when he left, the Tipperary man stopped. "Jesus," he told me, "I just looked at myself, and asked what am I doing this for? Sure I could never play like him." He said that he used to bring a clean shirt to work for Joe some days because Joe would always be going off to play somewhere at night.

It was like there wasn't enough air for him to breathe in Ireland or England so he left for America. There's a photograph of him at the airport; he looks strong—muscular—his overcoat hardly able to contain him. I look at that photograph and I imagine the breadth of his shoulders, the breadth of him swinging into "The Wise Maid" or "Ships Are Sailing." When he came back he'd shrunken into the same overcoat and you'd wonder if it was a different man. It was only when he settled the Paolo Soprani on his knee, the cigarette in his mouth, that you knew and he knew himself how little time he had left.

One way or another he gave an idea of music to people that never went away. It comes back to me when you listen to that recording he made, comes back in such a way it's hard to listen to anyone else playing those tunes without comparing them to Cooley, and they're not often as good.

People will always talk about the different styles in music—the Galway style and the Clare style—but round here, where we near-on border with Galway, the two styles are the one. Both have, even in fast rhythmic playing, the same lonely notes. The border is an invisible boundary that has little effect on people's everyday lives. A musician doesn't decide to roll a note differently because, by

a fluke of geography, he was born in one parish and not another. The repertoire is a common one in both counties and you'd rarely hear a musician insisting he was from one place and not another—unless, of course, there was a hurling match being played somewhere. It's the same in other parts of the country: Leitrim and Sligo; Leitrim and Fermanagh and Cavan; Sligo, Mayo and Roscommon; Cork and Kerry; and the whole of the north of Ireland has a fine vigorous fiddling style that has much in common with Scotland. Counties were an English invention. They would never have worked, only for the GAA—the football and hurling teams that gave them identity. To some people anyway, the county team would often come after the parish team. We always seem to end up back at the parish. The old *Clare Journal* once carried as a headline beneath its masthead: LOCAL MAN DROWNS AT SEA. Titanic Sinks.

In that way a musician like Cooley would feel at home here. Not that a musician like Cooley, or any decent musician, wouldn't feel at home anywhere music was played. Tom Power was another Galway man who had a great influence on the music in these parts. Power was music-mad. He worked in a garage in Crusheen. He was the first man I met who could note-read. He taught himself. For most musicians that was like learning to read in the first place. If they went about it at all, they'd do it in a halting manner, as if they were spelling

the words out to themselves. Power wasn't like that. He could have read music of the turns in the road.

At that time, in the 'thirties, Frank O'Higgins had a program on the radio. O'Higgins would play music the likes of which we'd never heard before, music from all over the country. Sometimes a phrase or a piece of what he played might stick in your mind and you'd be going round humming it, trying to imagine what was missing. O'Higgins had a grand, clear, unornamented style. He was a good teacher. You'd pick up the music from him by degrees. If you were lucky you might hear him play the same piece a few weeks later and it would all fall into place, but mostly you'd be frustrated and the piece would eventually slip from your mind.

One day I was passing through Crusheen and I went in to see Power. I'd heard O'Higgins playing a strange tune on the radio the Sunday before. It was called "The Good-natured Man" and I couldn't get it out of my head, but the furthest I could get in it was the turn. I knew Tom had a good ear for unusual tunes. He was under the bonnet of a car and when I came into where he was working he emerged, a big grin on him, his face streaked with grease. I asked him if he'd got that tune.

"Come with me," he said, and I followed him out. He told me to pump the water up as he

Connemara haystacks.

washed his hands. He wiped them on his overalls and went back inside. When he came out he was carrying a brown paper parcel. He unwrapped a big green book called *The Dance Music of Ireland—1001 Gems* by Francis O'Neill. All we ever called it after was "O'Neill's Book" and then "The Book."

Power and myself pored over it. It was like morse code to me, but there were so many tunes in it, tunes with great names like "Douse the Monkey," "Upstairs in a Tent." Tom would open it at a page, study it for a minute, then whistle the start of something. He gave me the turn in "The Good-natured Man." All of us in the area started playing it and when the Tulla Band took it up it was played all over the country.

So it was Chief O'Neill of the Chicago Police Force who had the greatest influence on our music at that time. I never learned to note-read myself. In a way, I suppose, the music written down on the page looked to me like a dug-up skeleton. For to be able to read the music didn't mean the reader could play it. The knowledge of the music came from listening and letting it take control of you, letting it find its own direction. A reader, taking what was on the manuscript alone, would give every note the same stress. The tune might have drive but not swing; it wouldn't have the little twists and turns that make each playing different, each playing the making of a new tune. The written

The Wheels
of the
World

Tommy Peoples and Paddy Mullins. Peoples has arguably been the most influential player of traditional music in recent years. For many he is the greatest fiddle player of his or any other generation. An original member of the Bothy Band, he appeared on their first album "The Bothy Band 1975." He recorded two albums as a solo artist: "The High Part of the Road" and "The Ironman," as well as an album with Matt Molloy and Paul Brady. A native of Donegal, his playing displays amazing technical ability allied to subtlety, virtuosity, and something—in those musicians who have it—which defies description: at his best, and he invariably is, his music carries a great emotional charge. Paddy played the flute with the legendary Kilfenora Céilí Band. In the early days of the fleadhs, competition between the Tulla and the Kilfenora bands was eagerly awaited, and nowadays has taken on the stuff of legend. On one occasion the bands were adjudged to have drawn and were asked to play again; Kilfenora was given the title by half a mark.

notes were the bare bones that a good player could ornament. Somebody sent back sheet music from the Cavan fiddler Eddie Reavey, who lived in Philadelphia. We'd been playing some of Reavey's tunes for years, without realising that their composer was still alive and still composing.

O'Neill's book, his *1001 Gems,* was like a bible to us. It's still called "The Book." People that it might as well have been Greek or Latin to, or the writing you sometimes come across on ancient standing stones, boasted of having a copy of it in their house. O'Neill fixed the music that had been in people's heads—someone notated it from his playing and in this way he saved hundreds of tunes though he couldn't write music himself. He was the first man that truly translated the imaginary standing stones and made sense of them. When you hear politicans and the like on about great men and patriots you never hear his name mentioned, but to my mind he was a great man and a patriot. There is no monument to O'Neill, no street named for him, but then he created his own monument and it's alive in the air every day of the year in every corner of the world.

Music was with me every hour of the day. When I was working there'd be tunes in my head. I'd wait for the fairs because it was there that you'd hear the rambling fiddle and accordion players. I was beyond in Spancilhill at a fair once. I hadn't my fiddle with me as my excuse for going

was to look at horses. Look I did, but I bought nor sold nothing. The only spitting I did on my palm was to make sure the bottle didn't drop from it.

I was on my way home when I heard this strange music. I was drawn towards it, for I'd heard nothing like it before. The tune I knew—it was "Johnny Allen's Reel." Johnny Allen was a fiddle player from beyond Feakle and he's still talked about even though nobody can remember directly playing with him. But it was the musician that drew me.

I caught sight of him through a sheet of canvas drawn out in the form of a windbreak. From my side of it all I could make out was a shadow, like a ghost almost, playing pure wild driven music, as if there were no one there, just an elbow pumping the bellows. I asked someone who he was and they said his name was Johnny Doran and that he was a travelling man and a piper. There was a crowd drawn up about him and that was the only way I ever saw him, in the middle of a crowd at fairs and at football and hurling matches, anywhere there was a crowd.

From that on I always looked out for him whenever he was about this way. At the other end of the county the appearance of Doran was enough to make Willie Clancy lay down his hammer and saw. Doran could never play the same piece of music the same way twice. He was inventive in his twists and turns and sometimes he didn't even recognize that a tune had a natural conclusion. He'd loop it round in a circle, launching into it again and again, and each relaunching was a completely different creation. You could never ask what setting of a tune came from Johnny Doran; he had so many he wouldn't even remember them himself—for him the music just happened. His playing had in it echoes of the time the old man who taught me had talked about, when the whole country was alive with pipers; and hadn't Doran's family links back to those times, wasn't he descended from the Cashs, themselves horse dealers and pipers?

And when I thought about that it made the music seem ancient for me—ancient and, in a way, biblical. I would think of that part in the Old Testament that I used to read from the big American bible we had above in the house, the part where they all beget each other. I would think of Doran, the brother of Felix Doran the piper, the son of John Doran the piper, himself the grandson of the piper John Cash and nephew of "the star piper of the whole globe," James Cash. And then the Cashs were mixed in with the Rowsomes, another great family of pipers.

Even though I heard other good pipers after, none had his volume—he was used to debating with noisy crowds. Debating and winning. Even now, if I close my eyes, I can still see the great Doran buckling on his pipes, launching into a set

of tunes the likes of which you'd never have heard before—and never will again, for Doran died from injuries he suffered when a wall fell on his caravan in 1948. But anywhere there are crowds of people gathered in good humor, then the spirit of Johnny Doran is there laughing with them, his music making them see things in themselves they didn't know were there. Freeing them into reckless laughter with reckless, passionate music. Johnny Doran playing the great music.

I'd travel anywhere I was asked to play, and play in any company. I'd play for a shilling or a cup of tea or for nothing at all and steal a cabbage from a garden on my way home if I was hungry. We wound up at a house-dance once, Corrys was the name of the place—myself, Tom Power and John Joe Cullinane. That was the first time I ever saw Paddy Murphy playing the concertina. I remember because he was playing with his brother who went to England after and he didn't know our tunes nor we his. We played every second turn all night, me and Power and Cullinane, then Murphy and his brother. He said to me it was the first night he'd come across so many tunes. He was only from Connolly, a few miles away, but people didn't travel much then unless they had to. Cars weren't too plentiful then.

There was a crowd of us playing over in Kilaneane once. The curate there, Father Clune, was a native of Crusheen parish. There was Willie

Halloran, Patrick Devanney, Mick Preston Young, Mick Preston Old and myself. They had sports and a dance at the school after. They made a dancing platform. There was no amplification; we just played at our own steam. I went outside—there wasn't many places had inside toilets then, never mind in schools—and I was walking round the side of the school and there was an auld man. I suppose he was older then than what I am now. There he was up against the window and his hand up against the glass to cut down the glare. He had an auld stick, a blackthorn stick. The boys were playing inside the window and he took to playing the flute on the stick outside, copying what they were playing, fingering and all. He kinda knew. I went up and I tapped him on the shoulder. "O God," says he, "there's great music in there."

"Whyn't you come in?"

"I couldn't come in and them collecting money in there," he said.

Anyhow, I brought him in. There were a couple of tables and a stage fitted on top of them and I landed him above on it, playing along with the rest of us. One of the Prestons gave him a flute. He hadn't them all but he had some of our tunes. He was in heaven.

Seán Reid came round these parts as an engineer with the county council. He was from up the north. Reid played the pipes himself but it was as an organizer that he was outstanding. He'd go to

any lengths for music. At one time he took the county council to court over his job. They threatened him with losing it if he didn't give up the music. The music wasn't always respectable. Reid used to say, "It's no matter a jot how bad a musician is, especially if he's a middlin' auld fella, you'll always learn something from him, another tune or a tune in a different setting." And that was true, for without the people who kept it alive, both good and bad musicians, there would be no music. Without the man who took up his fiddle to scratch out a few tunes at the end of his day's work, or the woman, like my own mother, who took the time to show her children how the different sounds were made, the only notes that would be on the air would come from the birds.

The country house-dances were our school. It was there you learned to play music and to dance and to sing, and where you'd meet your girl, if you had one. All the music was played at country dances. You'd travel all over the locality, maybe playing at the odd parish hall, school or sports day. If you were a half-good musician it would be known you were playing at such a house and people would follow you from one place to the next. There'd be nights in it and they'd be knocking sparks off the flags, tripping over one another in the effort to dance. Some houses would have an upturned pot set under the flag by the fire. You could hear the echo from it. The good dancers, and often the bad dancers, would head for that flag. Everybody would be listening for the wayward step or the dragged foot. Bad dancers could make awful fools of themselves taking the flag before the fire. The kitchens were small and if the next four stood up while the first four were finishing off there'd be a crush on the floor. There'd be maneuvering going on to get two good dancers on the floor for the same set; then they'd rival one another adding their own modifications to the figure, calling for their own preferred tunes. People would be clambering up on seats and over the table to watch them, urging them on, roaring and shouting and clattering and battering.

Then, at the end of the night as the dancers drifted home, there would be talking and singing. The singers would sit in a circle, swapping songs, sometimes until the cows came home—or the man of the house, or maybe his wife, rose to drive them home. There was always work to be done the next day.

Songs were like tunes and a good singer could write a song to match a great occasion; there were songs of loss, songs of mourning that had the ochón, the note of sorrow that came from the music or from the Irish; there would be songs to celebrate football or hurling matches, songs about battles, love songs and songs of rebellion, and humorous songs celebrating a cow getting stuck in a bog or a drunken man getting lost on his way home from his revels.

Michael Considine fell in love with Mack the Ranger's daughter beyond in Clooney but, being from a big family and not having money, he emigrated—to America. There he wrote a song called "Spancilhill." In it he dreamt, like many's another, that he had travelled back home again. One way or another there was always a lot of travelling done in dreams. "Spancilhill," with all the sentiment and emotion in it, became very popular. And no wonder, for isn't it a true song? Isn't it those who are exiled who have those sentiments as they lie in their beds at night listening to the sounds that are made in a city? And are they not entitled to them?

the Heartbeat of IRISH MUSIC

My Love Is In America

Seán Tyrell. Seán comes from Galway. A fine singer and interpreter of songs, he is known for his diverse and unusual repertoire and his powerful, emotional delivery. His album, "Cry of a Dreamer," is seen as a landmark in the recording of Irish songs, and his live performances linger in the memory for a long time.

Then the years of the dancing came to an end. The years of mad battering dancing which, if you were caught in the middle of it, you'd think would go on forever, one night leading into the next as sure as one figure followed another. And when it was over all that was left was the memory of it, the way you'd remember the light a lamp gave off after it was quenched. And the way it happened left something in the air like the whiff of paraffin that lingers on after the lamp was put out.

The forces that eventually finished the dancing had been drawn up against it for years. For as long as anyone could remember the dancing, they could remember the priests condemning it. Not every priest, mind you. There were musical priests and priests who came from musical families and priests who knew that the people deserved any small distraction they could get from the hardship of their daily lives, priests who tried to harness the energy in the people and who saw that energy in the music and dance. Not every priest could be blamed, but the Church was behind it. They seemed to have a policy on it that went back into the last century. Dancing, they said, was an occasion of sin—anything they couldn't control was an occasion of sin.

In the 'thirties there came a new type of music into the country. Dance bands came down from the cities playing waltzes and foxtrots on drums and trumpets and saxophones that had only been seen before in the brass bands in one of the towns, huffing and puffing. An old man told me it was like the days of Father Mathew's Temperance Movement—that was when the brass bands first appeared and many's the musician thought then that it was the end of our own music. A fiddle player couldn't compete with the noise they could strike up, frightening the birds of the air. Private dance halls opened up all over the country. The dance-band music caught on like wildfire; it was loud and fast and it was American—we seemed poor value by comparison.

The battle with the clergy was an old one. They'd almost done away with the crossroad dances. One might be held on St. John's Eve, with the priest on the lookout—or a lookout on the priest. There were stories, from all over the country, of the priests hunting in the ditches with their blackthorn sticks after a dance. Some say the people were priest-ridden. But the people could make up their own minds—after all, dancing had survived everything the clergy threw at it, and the people never stopped dancing. It was the government that handed the clergy the tool that finished off the country house-dance.

During the economic war of the 'thirties, when Éamon de Valera's government withheld the land annuities from England and the English retaliated by imposing duty on Irish cattle exports, survival for the smallholder was from hand to mouth. Cattle were down to shillings in price; it was often easier to kill the calves than to feed them through the winter. But rents and rates still had to be paid.

People had always pulled together. There was the old system of working the land, the system where everyone—men, women and children—would weigh in to help their neighbors with the hay or turf, and be, in turn, helped themselves: the meitheal it was called. What happened during those years of the economic war was just an extension of that system. It had happened before during the land war when people drew together to fight evictions. It was the system whereby you never gave up on your neighbors.

Houses ran card-drives alongside the house-dances. They might charge sixpence or a shilling entry, depending on whether there was a supper, and a goose or turkey would be played for. The proceeds would pay the rent or rates, and the card-drives moved around the houses as they were needed, my turn tonight, yours tomorrow. After the cards there followed the music. In this way many's a man and his family was saved from the road or from hunger.

In 1936 the government introduced the Public Dance Halls Act. Plenty of politicians have since said that it was only meant to control the big, private dance halls. The government was making nothing from this dance boom, but private dance hall owners were growing rich. Now dances were to be regulated and a tax of twenty-five percent was introduced. Soon the Church forced its way onto the bigger dance floor—parish dance halls were built which they had control of and any priest who liked could use the Guards to harry the house-dances out of existence. And that was what happened. Houses where dances were held ended up in court and their owners were fined. Tom Considine was taken to court and fined ten pounds; he hadn't even made five pounds the night the dance was held in his house. After years of coercion, of opposition to the house-dances, the Church now had the means to end them.

And they went about it in the right way. They played every card they had. House-dances were illegal, they said, occasions of sin, and they even accused us of raising money for the IRA. For myself I had no interest in politics and knew no one who claimed to be in the IRA, but I was denounced from the altar, I was threatened with excommunication—maybe I was excommunicated for all the difference it made to me. Some of my neighbors began to avoid me or to talk in low voices when I passed them. All of a sudden I was supposed to be out with a gun.

The only history or politics I knew had to do with the music. I had supported de Valera because he promised to do away with the annuities, because I thought it was wrong for us to pay England for land that was ours. I was a young lad, playing music on the street the night in Tulla he interrupted his speech and bowed his head to say the Angelus, but then I'd probably have played music for the divil himself and not have noticed, if the tunes were good.

Politics and history were things people wrote about on the roads—vote for this one and that one—and those writings got weathered and wore off and the political parties fell out among themselves or took new names. I would still have to struggle after a plough, bouncing across rocks, trying to get purchase with hardly the weight in my body to bear down on it. From where I stood, mostly in the bottom of a drain, armed only with a dredging fork, what was written on the roads or who did what in Dublin changed nothing. But the Dance Halls Act destroyed everything.

When I look back on those times, it's like looking at faded photographs of old family excursions. I feel a great sense of loss that so much of what was good was so carelessly ended. I thought then I was hearing the death rattle of the music itself. When my father was carried into our kitchen on the door my mother held a small mirror over his face to see if there was life in him. Then my mother died soon after. She died a sad death, her body riddled with disease, crying out for my father in the middle of the night. The night before she died she crawled her way from the bed out into the kitchen. It was the dead of winter and there was snow on the ground. "Why aren't you out ploughing the field in front of the house?" she said. I didn't know what to do. So I hitched up the horses and went ploughing in the winter snow, stumbling like a child behind them as Tom tried to lead her back to her bed. Both of us crying.

I had lost hold of everything. Tom was getting ready to leave for America. He was taken up with the excitement of it. "Come with me," he'd say. "We'll lease this place out in conacre. If you don't like it you can always come back." I felt old then. Too old for America. Maybe my life's hap-

At the end of a great seisiún one Friday night in Newquay—Paddy Hardiman and Vincent Gaynor.

pened in reverse—as the music again got popular in the years ahead, I started to feel younger. But then I was for staying. I didn't think I'd feel the music as much anywhere else. I wanted to witness what was happening to the country.

And then came the times like bad dreams. It was like we were living and moving underwater, so slowly was everything happening. It was the custom then that when someone died belonging to you there would be no music in the house for twelve months, nor would anyone from the family play anywhere else. I felt, the day I hung up the fiddle in the kitchen, that it was final. I would never play music again. I remembered how my aunt, a fine fiddle player, had stopped playing when her mother died. In the eleventh month of her mourning her husband died and she never played a note again.

I used to go abroad in the fields at night. I could hear the music wafting towards me, the waltzes and foxtrots. I couldn't understand the attraction a band down from the city for one night could have. It seemed to be calling me, but I couldn't understand that either. It seemed to be saying: This is England, this is America.

After the twelve months, there were tunes I'd nearly forgotten about. I used to go up to my old teacher's house. He was old and frail then

My Love
Is In
America

and on his way out, and all we did was sit and talk about the past. Only for another neighbor of ours, Michael Talty, who was a flute player in his young days, the fiddle would still be hanging there.

"Take it down. Take it down," he'd say. I'd have cows to milk and jobs to do but I'd steal out and come into the house and play a few tunes for him and every one of those tunes would be like the last one. Everything was spinning away from me. The world was passing me by. All the old musicians I knew were dying and the younger ones emigrating; soon there would be nobody left to play with. Soon there wouldn't be enough men left alive to carry out the dead.

But it was the women who left first. They could look forward to better lives in England and America, away from the drudgery of farm work and the narrow lives they'd be forced to live in the small towns. They started to go wholesale during the war. There was work for them in the munitions factories, and nurses were needed in the hospitals. The men that were left often couldn't look forward to much, they'd be broken in two and lucky to get married at all. They used to say that Lisnamac was cursed from the Famine times, cursed that no birds would sing there. But I knew better than that. The curse was a modern one—even if it was one we'd known for long enough—the cries of children weren't to be

heard. And the ones who left were the ones who hungered for change. We were resigned to it all and we had no way of expressing it. At my grandfather's wake my father said the women keened for three days. At my father's wake we stifled our grief. Nobody threw themselves on coffins anymore. We had forgotten how to keen or maybe we had grown used to it or we feared what the sound of our keening might be like. Even after they left we held it in; we lit candles for them, waited on their letters, the odd few pounds here and there that made things easier, the money for the slates, the grand—but regretful— tombstones they might erect above us.

I was asked to play at an American wake one night. It was in Taltys. Teeney, the youngest daughter from a house that had once been full, was leaving for Boston. I'd played, near enough as a child, in that house, when the first of them left and Mick insisted I come over. The Taltys were no different a family than any of the rest of us. They lived in the same sort of house we did, farmed the same bad land. I remembered the bits of the pig hanging from the ceiling. Every-thing they produced they devoured themselves.

I sat in the corner waiting to be asked to play, for old times' sake. The memory on me of an old man, three or four times my age. People always make out that memory is a great thing— well it's a burden and a curse. It often felt to me that I was bearing the memories of other people with me as well as my own, as if I was carrying the memories of times I couldn't have lived in. I was too young then to feel that way.

I played for myself that night. I played the reel "My Love Is in America" over and over, scouring it from my memory. Like Doran I hungered for the one tune. The other musicians gave up trying to follow me. The dancers gave up on me. Everybody sat round listening to me play, watching me. It was the first time in my life so many people had done that when I played. All I could see was a sea of faces but I couldn't recognize any one of them definitely. All I have now is the memory of being there. It was like the old man had said: the turn in that tune just burst from me and everything exploded into yelps and whoops about me. I could see the music running in fast colors before me and I felt it run, like voltage under my skin, riveting me to the chair.

After a while I found a tempo, settled into it and the man beside me took up the flute and joined in. The dancers took the floor again. They battered and thundered and for a while it was like the house was about to heel over. The teacups were rattling where they stood. It was like, with the door closed there, it might go on forever, as if the force of the music could stop time itself. When the tune did come to an end they gathered around me, panting with exhaustion. The old woman of the house said I was every bit the fiddler my uncle who disappeared to America was.

"It doesn't grow on ditches," they said.

"Jesus—that was some playing."

"Boys O boys, but he can make it talk."

But it wasn't me at all. It was there in the room with me. It was everybody else. It was all of us.

The house was done up to the knocker that night. Everything polished and gleaming. That house is empty now. They went outside to see that girl off at seven in the morning, laughing and crying. That was a girl I always had a fancy for but could never say it. I would think of the foxtrots and what a poor fool I was. I would always remember that morning. It was drizzling and, as she climbed into the car, the drizzle shrouded her face like a mantilla.

The whole country was empty of laughter; it was like sitting alone, at night, in a house buffeted by wind. Maybe it was that when times were good I was too occupied to notice how bad things were. Maybe all I ever saw was the music. Maybe it blinded me. Maybe a pig is only happy in muck when the weather is warm. At any rate I had my fill of rocks and drains and I was for leaving.

My Love is in America . . .

My Love is in America . . .

The Brown Coffin

In the 'forties and 'fifties, after the war, there was plenty of work to be got in England. There was work the length and breadth of that country on motorways, hydro power stations, dams, airports and in the towns. I left Altandown in '47, when the war was two years over and the great effort to rebuild England in full swing. I headed first for Manchester where I had cousins, and I was working the morning after

Jack Broomhead's wake. Jack was a Yorkshireman, drawn to east Clare by the music; he moved to Feakle some years ago. By trade he was a plumber and by inclin-ation a banjo player. He died tragically young. This photograph was taken in the kitchen of his house on the night of his wake. The fiddle player is P. J. Hayes, founder of the Tulla Céilí Band and a friend of Jack's.

I landed there. Then I took up with Murphy the builder, digging trenches and laying post office cable. Well-paid work at that time, some of the best work there was.

The last thing I did at home was to dig the grave of the man who taught me music. If anyone asked why I left that was what I'd say—I left home over the digging of a grave. Not that anyone would ask. We were all over there for the work, and you took the work and the money that came with it, where you could get it. The only difference was I still owned twenty-eight acres of land, and I wouldn't tell that to too many. A few acres of land—even bad land—would start to look good to a man that gave years on the roads over there, travelling from job to job. The land was in conacre. I told the auctioneer to pay the money into a bank in Ennis and I took the bank book and sent it to Tom in New York. He could have whatever use he wanted from it—that money wouldn't do me any good.

With Murphy, in those days, you had to be willing to travel. I was made up to ganger man and given my own gang of men. We worked the belt of country above the midlands, from Cheshire across to Lincolnshire. We were in Nottingham for the Goose Fair and came down through small towns with names like Cowlit and Crowland. One day, as we were digging out trenches along the road, we were showered in spuds and clods of earth and we found a gang of Mayo men working in the fields. They heard our accents and we stopped to talk to them, shouting up from the trenches, encouraging them to desert for a better life with us. They were seasonal workers, over for the few weeks it would take to harvest all of that part of the country. They were mostly family men, with

wives and children looking forward to the extra money over the winter months. One of them was a flute player. Grogan, I think, was his name. Flute players, I used to think, had the right idea; you could pull the instrument apart and stick it into your pocket. It must have been the first time reels were heard in a field in that part of the world. We sat in the shelter of the ditch then and he played the jig "Miss Monaghan," and the way he rolled the notes and the pattern of his breathing between them would stick in my mind for a long time.

From there we turned in a southeasterly direction, heading first to Murphy's yard in the town of Ely. As we drove down into Norfolk the spire of Ely cathedral rose out of the mist before us, out of the flat ground from where the sea had been driven back. You could imagine the tide marks still on the land. Sea mists drifted far inland. Everything was the grey color of ash trees in winter. Water leaked everywhere, into drains and canals. I had no fiddle with me any-more. All I could do was imagine music. I felt the way ancient sailors must have felt, back in the times when they thought the world was flat and that they were sailing towards the edge of it. Only that I seemed becalmed—just short of what, I didn't know.

But even then I should have known I'd had enough by the time we dug Hughie

Cailín's grave. I should have jacked it all in and gone home then, but I didn't. It rained all day, the day we dug Hughie's grave. They had, in the English system of things, men employed to dig graves, but we insisted we'd do it ourselves; it was the least we could do—it was all we could do.

When I met Hughie I was a ganger. One morning Tom Sullivan, the contracts' manager, called me into the office and told me I had a new man for my gang. Sullivan would go through the country ahead of us, setting up a yard somewhere. He would be responsible for several gangs on price work, like ourselves, and more men on day work. It was the day-work gangs that occupied him—they were where the money was, booking in what we called "dead men" and picking up several wage packets for himself at the end of the week. I had no liking for Sullivan. He knew that, but as long as the work was done and, from my end, we were paid on time, we tolerated each other. With the hunt for day work we never saw much of him anyway and when we did he was usually burning his shins in an office somewhere, his bad eye rolling like a loose marble in its socket, he slithering around like a mound of jelly across a plate. Someone once said, when he did come out to where we were working, that we should tie a tin can to

his tail and send him back where he came from.

"I have a new man for you," he said. I asked was he any good. The best, he assured me, the best. I could see all the other gangers were smiling at each other and I knew there was something I wasn't being told. But it was a Monday, I was the worse for wear, and I didn't question him. It was cold weather that time of year and I drove out to the job with Hughie in the back of the open wagon with three other men. Anyone who wasn't in the cab would be blue with cold by the time we got to where we were going. It was all price work, spade, shovel and fork work, and the theory was that a man blue with the cold would work all the faster to warm himself up.

I couldn't see what the problem with Hughie was. He was digging like a machine. Monday was always a day when there was little done. You'd make a showing. By the middle of the day all the men with bad heads were primed to go for the cure. I went with them. Hughie stayed where he was; he didn't drink. When we came back we stood and marveled at the amount he'd dug out. It was all well trimmed and bottomed. It was only when I picked up the drawings that I noticed Hughie had gone off in the wrong direction. With the day darkening and the time spent in the pub, by the time we'd back-filled what Hughie'd done we'd

Greg Daly, Brian Rooney, Lamond Gillespie and Dermot Grogan on Good Friday morning, the Fiddler's Elbow, Kentish Town, London. Brian and Greg are both from Leitrim, Dermot is a Mayoman, and Lamond is from London, by way of a Scottish father and French mother. Brian lives in London and isn't much recorded, but his music has had a great influence on London musicians like Lamond and on John Carty's fine album "Last Night's Fun." This was one of those special nights—perfect music that you'd think would go on forever, one of those nights that always has echoes in your head. It did end when they went out into the rain at seven in the morning, swearing they were all sober, still talking about tunes.

made nothing.

I didn't see Sullivan again until the weekend.

"How's Hughie doing?" he asked.

"Grand," I said, "Sure he's a great worker altogether."

"I know he can work," he said, "but you have to watch him all the time. He's a bit simple."

"I wouldn't have thought that now," I said.

Hughie had a single-row melodion and it went everywhere with him. I asked him what the music was like in Monaghan, where he came from. "Rough," he said. But when he played he could get all the men going. Laughing and yelping and lashing out with their boots at thin air. Buck-leppin' like summer calves, he used to call it himself. I asked him once would he not have traded the melodion in for an accordion. He said there was no use in carrying the extra row like a spare tire if you had no use for it. I was never sure whether he was playing some style of music I'd never heard before or whether it was just Hughie. Sometimes his music meandered off and you'd see that he was somewhere else altogether. It wasn't that Hughie was simple, he was just in another world all the time—one of his own devising. He was one of the few men I met, doing that kind of work, who had no taste for drink. Every Monday he sent money home—he never said what for. One time he asked me if

I played music myself, seeing that I knew so much about it. I told him I could scratch a bit on the fiddle. He was always at me to get a fiddle from somewhere and join him for a few auld tunes, as he called them. I never got round to it.

Murphy's gangers that time had a bad name. I was no saint myself; you wouldn't want to be if you were working with men who were called after animals—the horse, the bull and the elephant—but I was fairer than most and men stayed with me. Most of the men then had given years on the road, moving from job to job, living in big construction camps, trying to hang on to whatever they had of themselves; some of them trying to hang on to families. You'd see them in the huts at night, a war going on in one corner and a man writing home in another, ofttimes spelling the words aloud as he wrote: "Everything's fine here, a great life altogether." Keeping the old lie going. The big money. The great life. Men telling each other about the places they came from. You'd be hard pushed to keep anything of yourself. One time a Kilkee man asked me if I knew who owned a horse called "Spatter the Dew" that used to win the Kilkee Plate every year. Spatter the Dew was the name of a tune, but that showed what he was thinking of.

Hughie was with me two years by the time we reached that strange, flat part of the country. He died of another cold Monday, and he died

The
Brown
Coffin

when we all went off for the cure. I knew that day there'd be little enough work done. The men stood about in knots looking off across the fields. They could see the rain clouds gathering away in the distance, like a storm boiling up over the sea, and they were wishing it down on us. I was going to call the whole day off altogether but Hughie insisted he'd work on. If the rain came he'd find us in the pub.

When we got back there was no sign of him anywhere. We finished up what we had to do and were tidying up. Nobody was too worried. We thought he'd gone off for fags—it was a long walk to a shop. Then it was going-home time and we couldn't very well leave without him. The lads were spread out shouting his name when someone noticed the sleeve of a jacket sticking out of the trench where he'd been working. He was bent over double, as if he were looking for something he'd dropped, his arse and back in the air, his head and shoulders buried. We took him back into the village, laid out in the green, open-backed wagon we had. He died in a two-foot-six-inch deep trench because he hadn't timbered the sides of it; he'd died because he'd dropped his cigarettes. None of us ever timbered trenches at that depth. You never would, not on price work.

We didn't know what to do with Hughie then. Since we were all working under false names we didn't know if Cailín was his right name. We didn't know anything about him other than that he was from Monaghan. I got hold of Sullivan. "What can you do but bury him?" he said. "Many's a man was back-filled into his own trench and not a word about it." So we had a collection and bought a coffin and dug the grave ourselves because that was all we could do.

I thought of Junior Crehan's story about how they got that tune, "Caisleán Óir" or "The Golden Castle." At the time a crowd of men were digging a grave up at a place that overlooked a place called Caisleán Óir. It was a fiddler's grave. An old man came along the road and asked them if they had made the sign of the cross before they dug. They said they had. He told them the story of a priest who had taken a wife and was banished to live above the Cliffs of Moher. He was an Irish speaker that man, and he sang a song known as "The Priest's Lament." The air of that song stayed with them and a hornpipe was made from it and called after the place. I knew there'd be no music coming out of Hughie's grave, good soil and all as he was buried in.

Digging Hughie's grave reminded me of every grave I'd ever dug. The first one was the grave of a neighbor. There were three of us in it, Ownie, Patsy and myself. Patsy could dig.

Ownie was there as a distraction, to make sure the grave was the right size and in the right place. And I had never dug a grave before. I remember Patsy grabbing the shovel out of my awkward hands—he just snorted. He flipped over the top sods and began to dig as if digging were an end in itself. He flung the sods, rich with worms, back with ease. Patsy was a big man but, it seemed, there was no space so small he couldn't fit into it. When it came to my turn I had to jump down into the grave; it was like digging against the roots of a tree. The shovel kept flaking off bits of stone. I drove it down with my foot but, when I went to lever it back, the long handle caught on the side of the grave, tipping its contents over. No matter how I balanced, the same thing happened. Whatever spoil I did manage to throw out slid back in on top of me. Ownie said I was like a young lad trying to back an unwilling horse up to the shafts of a cart. When Patsy worked, the breath seemed to explode out of him as he hefted upwards. I muttered and swore under my breath as I rapped my knuckles and drove the blade of the shovel against my toes. We had an old graip which had been partly broken, and mended by tying a bit of a sack about it. When I went to use it splinters came through the sack into my hands. When we were going home that night Ownie said, "Look at the poor fiddler's

hands. Look at the hands."

By the time I came to dig Hughie Cailín's grave I was as good a man with the shovel as Patsy ever was. For some men that was a boast, but it was never like that for me.

There was no Catholic graveyard in the village where we laid Hughie to rest, so we buried him in the Protestant one. They had a corner in it for Catholics, off to one side, like the corners of graveyards you'd see kept for unbaptized children. One of the lads found what looked like the grave of a harper there, a headstone with the outline of a harp and the name worn from it. We joked that he would be in good company. Then someone wondered if we should have a separate burial for the melodion. But whatever laughter there was at that was uneasy.

A priest came out from Ely. He wanted us to take Hughie back into the town and sink him in the big Catholic cemetery there. I phoned Sullivan again; he said we were mad, were we going to be driving round the country with a body in the back of the wagon forever? So the priest did what he had to do and we left Hughie there to rest; the priest and the six of us at the funeral in the back room of a hotel.

The vicar in that church was a decent enough man and I asked him if he could get me the loan of a fiddle. We went back to a pub in the village. The man who owned it didn't know

The Brown Coffin

whether to be happy to see us or not—we were sure to spend an amount of money, but his other customers mightn't come in. It was late on in the evening before I took up the fiddle to play. There was great stiffness in my hands. I hadn't held a fiddle in five years. The one tune I can remember playing that night was "The Brown Coffin." It's the only one I can remember. I remember that my music didn't make much impression. The men were sullen, staring into their pints. It wasn't as if Hughie had been there because he wanted to be there; it wasn't as if he could go home at night or weekends. We did the best we could for him.

We'd worked all over the country up till then. We worked in places where we weren't welcome and in places where they couldn't do enough for you. We were in the ruins of Coventry and in open fields where, if there were a single bush it would have been some shelter in the bitter wind that blew. We would often have been better off to have been animals with thick hides and wide haunches to shelter behind. We worked, got drunk and fought; we lost men to marriage and homesickness and had men arrested for fighting and for wrecking pubs, but, up until that day, no one had ever died on us.

Áine McGrath, from Naas, County Kildare.

Myself and Sullivan had an arrangement whereby he'd drop the money we were due behind the pier of a gate on the Friday. I'd go up to pick it up. Nobody knew of that arrangement beyond ourselves. Sullivan would come round and measure up when the job was finished. It was then we'd get the balance of what we were owed. The Friday after we buried Hughie I went up there. On the way back I thought of taking the money and disappearing. I knew if I did I would get the blame and the men would be left short. You always heard stories about men who had done that and who were caught up with. I never knew anyone who was caught—stories like that had to be told. But it wasn't that that stopped me—it was just that it was something I'd never done before. Instead, I took the money back and paid the men out. Then I jacked. I walked away without even collecting what was due to me. I should have gone home then but I didn't. I headed to London. Then I got into the headings and started playing music again. The music would come and go. The music would always be there. I was convinced of that.

The
Brown
Coffin

The Camden Reel

Jim Philbin, a Connemara box player. Jim worked for some years in Australia and played music there before returning to London. This picture was taken on a Sunday morning in London. Sunday-morning seisiúns were legendary in London. Musicians would travel from all over the city to pubs like the White Hart on Fulham Broadway, and those over from Ireland for a weekend would look in in search of a few tunes. Anything could happen—and there was still a day ahead. Some of the spirit of this music is captured in the album "Paddy in the Smoke."

*T*he first place I hit was Camden Town of a Sunday morning. The heat of the sun beat the memory of that day into me. I walked up from Euston Station, my jacket slung across my arm, everything I owned—the twenty-eight acres apart—in the cardboard suitcase I was carrying. I felt light and free in the world. With the bundle of money in my pocket, I could have stayed on that train and gone anywhere.

If you were Irish—even if you knew nothing about London—you'd know about Camden Town. Back in Ireland, at the mention of London, people would ask you what it was like there. I'd never seen anything like it before. It was like a fair day in Tulla, only different. There were men and women with accents from all the counties, music pouring from every doorway, from the Brighton and the Mother Redcap, the Camden Head and the Blackcap. People walking between them with glasses of drink, calling to each other, talking about hurling and football and the places they came from. There was a man capering a jig on the pavement outside the tube station and beside him a man I knew. He was bent double in the middle of the road, blasting a reel from a mouth organ, a big crowd gathered round him, his glasses steamed up and his foot driving up and down like a jack-hammer. The crowd shouting for tunes.

"Play 'My Love is Fair and Handsome.'"

"Your love is fair and handsome," he shouted back and the girl, clinging to the arm of the man who'd asked, laughed, a deep-throated laugh, like gargling with honey and whiskey, that laugh.

I got talking to the mouth-organ player. I asked him if he went home often.

"If I get lonely," he says, "I just get the 31 bus down to Camden Town. Sure I'll never go back now. What's there for me?"

He wanted to know if I had the fiddle with me. I told him I didn't have a fiddle at all. I hadn't had a fiddle for five years. I asked him about work, was there any chance of a start? He said he was just a glorified tea-boy where he was working, but if I wanted some real work—the good money—he'd have a word with some Connemara men he knew that were music-mad. We made an arrangement to meet the following week and that was how I ended up working underground.

I had a bundle of money in my pocket. I fixed myself up with digs and the next day I went looking for a fiddle. I found a big, fancy shop with an array of them in the window. Inside I saw more bows in cases on the wall than I'd ever seen in one place in my life. I was trying one of them out, not playing, just weighing, balancing it in my hand, when a man came out of the back. He was as wizened as an old tree on the Burren, that man. He had on one of those suits with the wide shoulders and, with his narrow waist, if you'd hung him up there among the fiddles, no one would have noticed.

"Are you quite all right, sir?" he asked. He had a very strange way of talking but I passed no remarks of that. I would take a man as I met him. I told him I was looking for a fiddle.

"A fiddle, sir," he said. "And can you play?"

I took up the nearest one and played a snatch of an air and a reel. When I made to stop he waved me on like a man banking a crane. He'd never heard music like that before and him working only a mile from the heart of it. I told him he wanted to go up to Camden Town of a Saturday, or a Sunday even. He said he had just the fiddle for me, made by a Dublin man called Perry. I held it up with my ear against it and plucked the strings; the sound it made was as warm and mellow as the echo of music in a loft full of ripening apples. Even the ripple of the grain through it seemed charged with music. I felt that it was perfectly balanced, that I could play it without holding it—it would slip over my collarbone and under the bow. I wanted to send the notes flurrying through the shop, as if I were trying it out in a kitchen, bouncing them from the stone flags and the walls, but the shop was so big they just disappeared into the corners. Even though he gave me a good price on it and threw in a set of strings, by the time I'd bought the bow and case it cost more money than I'd meant to spend; it was like when I bought my first car, years later. As long as he was there, he said, he would service it gratis.

I spent the next few days walking the streets of Kentish Town, repeating the street names like a strange litany. I was one of those men who never learned to walk city streets. You see men like me, walking hunched over, head down, driving down into the pavement, as if afraid that if they strode out the ground would pitch away from under them, every step an act of balance. Men who could have navigated

where they came from by a bush, a broken branch or a tussock of grass, lost in eternal mazes of streets that all looked the same—willing themselves to learn their names.

One morning I wound up outside the old Catholic church on Lady Margaret Road. I went in and there was a Mass going on. You'd know by the look that they were mostly Irish women there. You'd know that by the cut of them, the way they held themselves. I thought of Altan-down and of the roads about there and I thought that, the music apart, religion was the only familiar thing to me in England.

What was left of the bundle of money was going fast and I needed work. There was work all right, long days compacted underground, hard up against another man's body and smells, driving tunnels through the bowels of London. Nothing in my head but tunes. Tunes and the thought of tunes keeping me going. My body working, tearing the muck out in reel time, then in jig time, just to keep my mind occupied—for what is work but the occupation of time and mind, and all the better if the mind can be kept out of it. Turning the same phrase over and over, as if there were a key in it, a secret that would make the playing perfect. As long as you didn't get on to the slow airs you'd be making money—it was all price work and, like Murphy's trenches, we were paid by the yard.

Worrying about the turn in "The Fox-hunter's," how to get that part to sound like baying hounds. The noises of the streets far above you, the noise of the compressor, belching air. The air gun rattling in your hands, your fingers scrunched on the trigger of it, eyes half-closed and your body leaning forward as if walking into a gale, on your knees. The air gun kicking. Kicking through your hands, up your arms and into your shoulder blades. Rattling the life from you. Never thinking the damage it was doing, how your hands would one day numb over the keys of a flute, stiffen like candle wax round the soundpost of the fiddle. Last night's fun, all right.

I was working mostly with a Connemara man, Coleen Naughton he was called. We gave years together in the headings and the longer I knew Coleen the more he surprised me. He was humped over with work. Working underground, there were six months of the year where you'd hardly see daylight, going down in the dark in the morning and coming up in the dark at night. Coleen was there, underground for years. The skin on his face was stretched tight and he looked as if he'd been preserved for centuries in a bog. He had the headings man's stoop, the pad of muscle at the back of his neck.

Coleen was the lead miner. There wouldn't be space for the two of us to work at the face of what we were digging out. One man would stage the other and the second man would see to the timbering, supporting the ground overhead with short scaffold boards, propped by struts, the boards driven ahead with a sledgehammer, the persuader. Above us, at the opening of the shaft, would be the crane driver, lifting out the skips of spoil. The tunnels were for everything, for the Ministry of Defence, for sewers, for the Post Office, for everything except that you would never ask what they were for; it was just a job, just work.

Lahinch, County Clare.

Whenever they talked about who built anything they mentioned the architect, they mentioned the firm, mentioned men who'd never dirtied their hands. You'd see plaques on the sides of buildings commemorating those men. When I first went to Camden Town the old men who'd been there all their lives used to talk about the building of the Northern Line. About how many men were killed on the cut from Euston station to the Underground station in Camden Town. That was the only way they were remembered.

You'd meet chippies—carpenters—who would write their names and the date on the back of a length of skirting or architrave before they fixed it. In that way they'd have some small claim to it, even if it was a secret one, known only to themselves.

The only way round Coleen was to start daydreaming reels again. He always had a riddle or a puzzle or a question of some sort on his mind. It used to drive me mad because he'd never give up till he got an answer that satisfied him. Somewhere along the line he got the impression that I was smart.

"What county in Ireland isn't touched by a county that touches the sea?" When he didn't get an answer: "Jesus Christ Almighty, that stuck you."

I was driven to imagining the maps on the walls at school. The big one when we still belonged to the empire, Ireland hanging like a red grace note off the edge of Europe, like a grace note ready to drift off at any time; and then the smaller map of Ireland itself, just green. I remembered the teacher pointing out the Burren to us and how I saw it, a series of brown cracks on the aged oil-cloth. I could see the Shannon standing out like the veins on the back of my hands. I imagined myself moving in from the coastline—and we'd made maybe two or three yards digging before I said, "Laois."

Whenever I remembered that map I'd remember Altandown, which wasn't on it, and I'd wonder briefly how was the land now? The conacre. The teacher showed us where we were on the map, but I could never work out why we weren't marked on it. The hill behind our house was the only mountain in my imagination then.

When Coleen found out I played music he wanted to know if the tune called "The Last House in Connaught" would be the first house if you were coming the other way. He didn't have any great regard for the music and I put that down to his being glad like many another to have escaped hardship and no money for a country where, at least, you got paid for the hardship—the music was in its way a reminder of that.

Even if I was music-mad myself I couldn't pass judgment on him for that. It put me in mind of other things. For most of us, just in talk even, the sea is a wondrous thing, but for Coleen it was a source of bitterness, the enemy of any man who tried to make a living from it in a small boat. It would be years before I got to see where he came from and, even then, I could only begin to understand.

The one time my father's brother Ownie, "The Yank," came home from the States, he hired a car and took us all to Lahinch for the day. I fell asleep on the way and woke to an ocean stretching before me. That was before I learned to recognize such things on maps, and the wonder I felt at seeing those acres of placid water never left me—whenever I think of the sea that's what comes into my mind. My uncle could swim and while he togged out my father

Antaine Ó Faracháin from Dublin. Antaine is a great sean nós singer and a collector of songs. He lives and teaches in Dublin and runs sean nós workshops all over the country. This shot was taken in the Fiddler's Elbow, Kentish Town, on a visit he made to London in 1992. Another early-hours seisiúm, to those who were around at that time the black circle in the background signals the absence of the clock, something that was never very much in evidence anyway. Peter Woods, author of this book, was the pub manager during the time these shots were taken.

rolled up his trousers and walked out, to his ankles, in the water. My mother strolled along the strand. She had her headscarf on and the wind was tugging at it as she walked. She looked to me like the last yellow blossom in a field of furze. Even at that time my mother was sick, though I was too young to know it.

There was a countrywoman there and I'll never forget her going out deep into the water in her shift, till it blossomed up around her, buoying her, and you could see the words "Ranks Flour" becoming visible across her back. Myself and my brother ran up the streets that day clutching the half-crowns our uncle gave us, amazed that no one asked us to hand them over. "Watch how you spend it," was all he said. It was the first time we had money of our own to spend. We bought the reddest apples we'd ever seen—it was also the first time we'd ever tasted tomatoes.

Later, someone in our house cut my mother's head from the picture of us all, sitting on a wall overlooking the sea, in an effort to see my uncle who was hidden behind her. That was the only photo of my mother we had.

I always had to work for what I had but, compared to Coleen, I could always afford sentiment. I was always rich in that way.

Then there were the weekends. You'd hold everything in you till the weekend and the weekend began of a Thursday evening. If you were on price work you'd expect to have your money made by Thursday. Friday you'd finish early. The music was the force that unified people—it didn't matter what county man you were if you liked the music. There were musicians in London from all over Ireland, learning new tunes, new styles of playing they'd never heard before. You'd hear people talking about them in the years to come; Séamus Ennis was there then and Máirtín Byrnes, Tommy McCarthy and Lucy Farr, Julia Clifford, Raymond Roland, Seán McGuire and Bobby Casey, Roger Sherlock and Danny Meehan, Liam Farrell and Brian Rooney. Some of them made names recording and some of them were never recorded.

There was the big Donegal man, one hand the size of the fiddle and still able to pluck "The Four Poster Bed" from the strings, or find the delicate notes in "The Japanese Hornpipe." There was the great Galway box player who had to join in every tune, even the slow airs. He'd have the box opening and closing, yawning with emotion, as if, at any minute, he was about to pull it to shreds, the notes dragged, almost squealing with pain from it. A profane man, a woman with a northern accent called him once—you'd never think a man like that could play music like that. And, almost as if he knew you were talking about him, he'd look up and wink and launch off into a reel, his head thrown back, laughing. There was the funeral of the Donegal man who fought to bring all his family up as musicians over there. Two days of solid music. Musicians from all over London and beyond, playing the styles of where they came from and, on the night he was buried, taking the stage in the workingman's club together and loosing such fast, demented music, they were like a céilí band from hell.

There were men and women from all over, from Kerry and Cork, from the west and north, and Claremen, always Claremen; you'd think when God said, "Let there be music," he'd added, "and a rake of Claremen."

That music was fast and loose, all the styles clashing together, fusing into a style of its own that was different from anything you'd hear at home. Music that just seems to bounce, that has great lift to it, as if each part of it is separately bouyant. For all the longing for home that music might give you, there were other things in it: a woman's long, lonely walk up a hospital ward at the dead of night, the pounding of jackhammers, boxes rolling from a conveyor belt before your face—always the momentum of work. It was the first time I'd known music to take that shape. It wasn't like the country-house music I was used to; musicians from other parts of the country didn't have to temper their music

to suit dancers. They played with greater vigor and at their own tempo. Over the weekend it would lift a burden from people, express something for them, releasing them for a moment or a night. You'd think of those pubs and of the talk, and the noise of glasses being filled and emptied. But in the middle of all that there was always somebody listening, a face turned up towards you. Maybe there was a memory for them in the music, a tune reminding them of a place or a turn in the road, or just reminding them.

For the music you had to go to the pubs. Most of the Irish were living in lodgings, but the Irish weren't too popular then so whatever chance you had of a bed you couldn't bring the music in with you. There were those signs everywhere: No Irish. No Blacks. No Dogs. Anyhow, more likely than not, the landlady would only know the two tunes. One would be "God Save the Queen" and the other wouldn't.

It was all in the pubs. There was the White Hart and King's Head, the Shakespeare and the Plough, the Eagle and the Black Cap.

There was so much work then you could always get a start up the road. I jacked four times in the one week on the Victoria Line myself, and went up the road for better money at the next shaft. Just bundle and go, as the Donegal man said. Just bundle and go.

Myself and Coleen were driving a heading out from under Victoria station. Above ground it was a wet Monday morning. Below ground it was always like a wet Monday morning, water seeping through the boards above your head; you'd be kneeling in it, condensation blasting from the air gun, your shirt soaked in sweat, buckets of steam rising from the man in front of you. But this day was different; it was Christmas Eve and we were working because it was a rush job—the pressure was on. The ground was worse than usual—wetter—and the going was hard. In any job we'd just tear into it but, on this job, there was no tearing into it. Two other gangs had jacked it in the previous week and we'd been offered a good price and the promise of a big bonus to put it right and finish on time. John White, who drove the small Jones crane, was late as usual that morning and Coleen was scalded with porter from the night before. We were slow in starting, unsure as to whether Whitey would bother showing up, and we were agreed to make a showing for a couple of hours and to head home early. In a way I was in no hurry. I was in a lodging house and I would be having Christmas dinner by myself.

One of the things we knew, without ever talking about it, was that you always checked the timbering that shored up the ground about you—always. Every man was, as they said, his

own safety officer. Safety officers weren't too common then and those that were there were often on the take. But, whether because of our bad heads or what, we didn't check anything that Monday. It was like the time I was nailing up a strut and I hit my thumb with the hammer. I turned to the man beside me and said, "Do you know, I knew I was going to do that and I couldn't be bothered stopping." He held up his thumb, the top of it missing. "I did that myself with a hatchet for the same reason," he said.

Anyhow, when we heard the snap and turned round we saw the roof behind us begin sagging in. We hadn't time to move before the lot collapsed, trapping us, and we couldn't blame anyone but ourselves.

We didn't know whether Whitey had even shown up and would be able to give the alarm that we were buried alive. We didn't know how much ground had caved in and whether we could dig back through it. We'd lost the air gun in the cave-in and only had a shovel with a cut-off handle and even if we could have dug, where would we have put the spoil? We were buried in a space barely longer than the two of us, flat on our backs. But more than anything else, we didn't know how long the air we had would last. I asked Coleen for his cigarettes. My own jacket was at the top of the shaft. Coleen had given up smoking but he

Jim Cerrigan's pipes. The uileann or union pipes are a wholly indigenous Irish instrument, invented in the eighteenth century. Perhaps because of this, piping can often seem like some arcane religion. Pipes made by pipe-makers in the eighteenth and early nineteenth centuries, such as those made by Kenna and Michael Egan who had a shop on Forty-second Street in New York, are highly prized, and the lives of pipers like James Handsey and Patrick Coneely have been detailed in Francis O'Neill's "Irish Minstrels and Musicians." In those days, pipers often enjoyed patronage— fifty pounds a year and the use of a horse was the norm, O'Neill tells us. But many pipers preferred the itinerant lifestyle, like the Dorans in more recent years. "Whimsical as prima donnas, pipers were always noted for their eccentricities," O'Neill wrote.

always carried twenty Capstan full strength in his pocket.

If we spoke to one another beyond that I could never remember anything more than us joking about Mick, the subbie we were working for, having to bring us down the Christmas dinner. I remember listening as the stillness settled about us. You could hear the hum of the traffic way in the distance like a far-off pot boiling. It was that city noise you got so used to you confused it with silence; anytime it wasn't there you'd lie awake at night listening for it. There was the sound of water dripping in from somewhere, each drop like a separate explosion. There were quieter sounds, as if the earth was breathing, lulling us to sleep.

I thought of dying in that space, buried in a grave we'd dug ourselves, myself and a Connemara man. Would anyone come for us? But I knew they would and then they'd bury me in a pauper's grave, since, for all that had happened to me, no one would know my right name. Mostly they'd just call me Clare, like many's another man called after his county. On paper I was Doran—I had taken the piper's name for my own. But I'd had other names—McMahon, for one.

I thought of all the names that had changed. The time the weather got cold up in the midlands, the ground hard and no outside work, and I'd got a job in a car factory pushing a brush. The first day there I saw my own cousin across from me on the assembly line. "Young Linnane," I shouted, "Young Linnane," and he raised his fingers to his lips: "For Christ's sake I'm called Daly here and I'm married with seven children if anyone asks." After that whenever I saw him I'd shout, "Young Daly, how's the wife and the seven children?" He used to avoid me. He still does to this day.

I thought and I knew Coleen was thinking of the two Donegal men that had been washed into a live sewer the week before, drowned because of a freak storm. When they came round in the pub, holding a collection for them, one of the men doing it told me they weren't a hundred percent sure where they came from. "We're still trying to contact relatives," he said. "They were both called Gallagher. We're all Gallaghers over here. Which Gallagher were they?"

I thought I could hear Coleen praying in Irish. I could hear his voice rising and falling in some strange rhythm. It was a while before I got used to it and then I knew he was singing. It was a sound I'd never heard before that day. In the maelstrom of the music that I'd been listening to and playing for years you'd hear the odd song, ballads mostly, sung in English, or the songs of John McCormack. I'd heard singing in Irish before, but it wasn't much different from singing in English beyond that you wouldn't understand it. Coleen's voice had an emptiness to it, a hollowness that you can try for but never really get into the music. There in the dark his voice and the song were the one thing. It was something that was in the language as much as in the singing, as if the language itself came from the depths of the earth. I found myself counting on my fingers as we used to do at school, counting the decades of the rosary. It was like he was praying as he sang and in the prayer the words and singing were one with the silences between them and the dripping water; like the part in praying where praying takes over and the beads just wind onwards between your fingers.

His voice had the same effect as the music did on me betimes. I could see Altandown and all the places round it. I could see the road turning from Tulla to Feakle. I could see places other men had described to me, the places they would think of when they thought of home, the mountains, rivers, lakes, and sometimes just the fields they returned to in their imaginations. I could see the place Coleen came from, how he'd told it to me, rocks and rock pools full of sea life and the sea itself, ebbing and sighing. I could see the place where we buried Hughie, the poplar trees at the edge of that graveyard, the dampness eating into his bones, the sea mists enveloping everything.

That song was something we had between us when they dug us out. It was like a secret you kept not because you promised not to tell it but because the telling of it might begin to unravel you. Maybe that was because the idea of it might seem strange or because, some might say, it was a waste of air and effort singing in the circumstances we were in. Coleen told me later that the singer of that song, "Caoineadh na dTrí Muire," was said to be guaranteed a place in heaven. He said he'd never sung it before but it was handy to have it around—it was like insurance. I thought of that often over the years, for Coleen wasn't what you'd call a religious man. I learned it later as an air, but I could never catch, in the playing of it, what he had. It was as if he knew it like a craftsman knows the hidden joins in the piece he's made and that piece is just furniture to anyone else. It remained an echo for me. An echo and a private place that reminds me of the time we were almost buried alive in a grave we'd dug ourselves; reminds me of that and of how time is in short supply. The time I was keened alive in my own language that I had hardly a word of.

By the time we got out of the hole that day the air was in short supply and both of us were gasping for breath. I saw Whitey's face above me, anxious, and apologizing for being late. "For Christ's sake, Whitey," I said, or so I was told, "it's the first time you've ever been on time." We lay gulping above ground like gaffed fish, the city air as sweet as any we'd breathed since the first lungfuls we'd ever taken. I heard the man we worked for saying to Whitey, "I'll have to send down two more dogs to put this right." He didn't speak to us. Whitey told us he said for us to take a couple of days off and come back when we were ready for work again. He said Mick wasn't the worst, he was one of our own. The two of them were from the same part of the country. Although myself and Coleen liked Whitey well enough he wouldn't have been our choice as a crane driver. The drink had a hold of him—he was always late or missing time. Yet we didn't object too much. We knew he was a sick man. He was always coughing and hawking up phlegm in a way that sometimes turned our stomachs, but we thought that maybe it was all the work he would ever get. In any case, the crane driver was down to the subbie—he was on day-work and all we could do to keep him sweet was to top up his wages with a few pounds of our own. Whatever parish or county fealty himself and Mick, the subbie, shared, we had no part of, nor no influence over. If we were soft on him we knew it would have done us little good to complain.

I knew Mick when he was on the shovel with Murphy and we all thought him a sound man. When he got the better work himself he changed. England does that to men, Coleen said. But it wasn't England. It was in him. Maybe some men might be reluctant to ill-treat their neighbors at home but when they got away they shook off those traces quick enough. He got heavy. He had lugs of skin on him like a baby and he dressed like he was poor. He hadn't an arse in his trousers and it was as if he hadn't the money to buy soap to wash the grease from the great lugs of skin. He stood there, his feet in his turned-down wellingtons, scuffling in the muck. "Bring me my shoes," he'd shout at Whitey. We used to invent curses for Mick: that he might die of scrofula, drown in a sea of greasy five-pound notes.

All that mattered to Mick now was that we weren't making money for him. When we weren't working we weren't paid. Many's the man had gone hungry the bad winter before that and Coleen had a joke about an Offaly man he knew who kept warm all winter, sweating he was, he said, and all he bought was the one bag of coal. He tied it over the bed and lay there worrying that it would fall on him. For all the jokes, Coleen had a family to feed and wouldn't be able to wait until he was ready to go back. Coleen, I knew, would be back at work straight after Christmas.

It was after that I thought of going to the States. Tom was doing well there, or so he wrote.

He was big in the bar business and America was a great place altogether. Tom always wrote to me even though the letters sometimes took months to catch up with me. He wrote to me even when I didn't write back. He wrote when he was on the ship over. He walked the deck of that ship every day, for miles. He was like my mother's old father, setting off, walking barefooted, on a half-demented pilgrimage to Lough Derg in the north of the country. He made the travelling real that way. When he got to New York he walked miles on a police beat and then he devised a system for betting on horses that made him his money. Then he bought the bars. He used to say that if you returned to Altandown with an English accent, even if you'd spent half your life there, you be looked down on, but after a wet weekend in New York it was all right to talk like a Yank.

I never got to America but I began to feel that I could have no more truck with England. It was like my body was there but a part of me had never emigrated. When I thought I might be dying, London never crossed my mind. The landscapes I saw were all of home and they had no people in them. What use was land without people? I was thinking of marrying then and the thought of bringing up a family there drove me to despair. I was thinking of marrying a woman I'd never spoken a word to, a woman I'd seen

only once but knew I'd see again. When I asked somebody her name they said, Mary Hynes. And so her face stayed before me and I used to comfort myself thinking of her, the way you might remember a sight of great beauty you glimpse from a train, promising yourself you'll go back one day, as the train throbs across the sleepers beneath your feet—Mary Hynes, Mary Hynes, Mary Hynes. Her name like the refrain of a song.

I wasn't like other men—all men tell themselves that, but I wasn't. I still had the land and there weren't many men who'd leave land that made sense to go out into a world that didn't. I was one of those who came and went, without weight. My passing would leave no impression. Camden Town would be no different without me. Somebody else would dig the tunnels. I could see my face in the faces of the old navvys I'd meet.

I had a thirst for drink I couldn't understand. When I wasn't working, I was drinking. I always thought I was in control of it because I never missed time at work. It stilled things within me. I was drinking to forget the room I was going back to—the threadbare carpet, the stained mattress, the alarm clock beside the bed. To forget the work I was doing—the big pour, thousands of cubic yards of concrete before you, pouring like grey pig's slop down the chute at you . . . the water and the muck. Diving into alcohol was like hitting icy water on a scorching hot day, freezing everything. Sitting in a pub at nine in the morning, the sun shining through the drawn curtains, half-thinking it was still night, flaking out reels, the music better because the drink had broken down something inside you. And then—maybe—one morning at nine o'clock you notice the dust on the optics and the smell of stale beer and the stink of the urinals in the air, and you're playing a different part of the tune than the man beside you, or a different tune altogether, and you're asking yourself, who do you know that you don't know from the pub?—and it's raining out.

All my playing had been in groups for years. I never played for myself. I never listened to what the music felt like, where it was going. The night we got out of that hole I took out the Perry fiddle again. I shut the door in the boarding house behind me and dragged the fiddle out from under the bed and the first reel I played was "Christmas Eve." Everyone in the house had gone home or had someone to go to for Christmas. I could hear the landlady in the flat downstairs battering with the brush on the ceiling to tell me to stop. I could hear her at her husband to go up and sort me out, but I knew

Joe and Biddy McNamara dancing the Lancer Set, which they taught at the Willie Clancy Week.

he was afraid of me. I didn't like people to fear me over the way I talked or the work I did, but sometimes it worked out that way and that was to my advantage. She was outside the door then, threatening to kick me out of the house. I tipped the chair-back under the door handle and began to play faster, wanting the music to take over my body like a sleeping draught. I could hardly feel the strings with the callouses on my hands. It was like playing with bandaged fingers. The music was only an echo outside of me. It was happening without me.

There was a tremor in my hand as I tried to play. I took out the bottle and had four shots of whiskey to settle it. Then I started to play every tune I knew.

I played my own tune. The one I had never played for anybody. It was as if there were a simple melodic line that was like a road, a road where I could find no turning off. I strained for the turn in it and it wouldn't come. It was full of false notes, so I switched over to other tunes. I played till I was back home in the trees. There was no light near me. It was dark as it had been underground, but I knew I was back in the trees, their rhythms brushing past me. I played so that I might disappear into the music.

The
Camden
Reel

the Heartbeat of IRISH MUSIC

PART TWO
from the fifties
to the seventies

Paddy Mullins.

Banish *Misfortune*

Josephine Marsh from Broadford in east Clare. The accordion, "the box," was once associated largely with male musicians, but Josephine is one of many women of her generation who is changing this. Playing in the east Clare style, she has released a fine album, "Josephine Marsh."

𝒯he first time I ever saw you," he said, when I asked him when he'd made up his mind he wanted to marry me. "That night in the Galty?" I asked. "No," he said, "the day I saw you outside the tube station in Camden Town. The day I first came to London and you were with someone else." The thing about it was I had no memory of being there—I mean, I could have been there—I was living there at the time. I just don't remember that day that's as clear as morning in his memory.

The first time I ever saw him was in the Galtymore up in Cricklewood, the night he was sitting in with the céilí band there. I had no great interest in the music then, I could take it or leave it, but I had gone there with Bridie Cashlin who had her eye on the drummer in the band. Bridie was famous for it—she always had her eye on some man.

I was looking at Eamonn, more

for want of something to do than anything else—I didn't want to get caught gaping up at the drummer with Bridie. We were standing before the stage, the clatter of sets going on behind us. I was wondering how someone could get so wrapped up in the music as that fiddle player when the round of tunes finished and I found he was looking straight back at me. I made to walk into the other part of the hall where the modern dance band was playing. He started from the stage after me and pulled at my arm.

"I know you."

"I don't think so," I said.

"Well, my name's Eamonn."

We got married in the church in Brook Green, Hammersmith, in April 1957. It was the first good day of that year—the clocks had changed and the sun drove the long shadows of the trees across the green until well into the evening; light poured through the big windows into the room above the pub that we went back to. The wedding was the greatest display of generosity I had ever seen in my life. Everybody brought something; everybody was involved in it—either preparing food or playing music. All our friends were there, the women I nursed with and the men he worked with and every musician he could get a hold of. More musicians arrived later in the day. They spilled from the small stage on to the floor.

On his way back from the altar he tried to hide a smile as he passed Coleen in the church. There was always more going on between them than I could understand—sometimes he'd look behind him, as if he expected Coleen to be there. "What were you laughing at?" I asked him later. It was over a suit. It was the first time Coleen had seen him in a suit. Eamonn hated suits and Coleen believed a man was only half-dressed unless he was wearing one, as well as a shirt and a tie. "Twice a year he goes up the Edgeware Road and buys a new one; he has more suits than I have trousers," Eamonn told me.

He was embarrassed in his suit, even though it looked good on him; he thought it was too grand, that blue suit with the red stripe through it you'd hardly notice. It was a present from his brother Tom. And you might have expected that not having seen each other for the best part of twenty years there'd be some awkwardness between them. I wanted to be there when they met and we got a taxi out to the airport. Coming back in they started to argue about some long-forgotten hurling match. Did you hear so and so died? I did—but wasn't he some hurler. He was all right but he was cowardly. Do you remember that game . . .

I liked Tom from the start. Eamonn used to say you'd think butter wouldn't melt in his mouth. He had a wide-eyed, generous and apparently innocent nature that America had done nothing to dampen—it had added to it—and his prosperity made him confident. Women who wouldn't have two words to say to Eamonn confided in him. They gathered round him to hear his wild tales of life in America.

"Do you know my cousin Maisie?"

"No, I don't think so. Where does she live?"

"Manhattan."

"Very fancy. The only time I was ever over that way was walking the beat. Did I tell you about the time, when I went over first, I was working with Whiskers Kelly, the longest-serving cop in the New York Police Department? Why, Whiskers fought on San Juan hill in '98 in the Cuban-American war, got special leave and came right back after. When Whiskers arrived in the city he didn't know his right hand from his left one. They took him down to City Hall, gave him a watch and a uniform and swore him in—he was directing traffic on Lexington the day he got off the boat. "Tommy," he said to me, "it took a while. I used to have to look down at my wrist to see which way left was.""

Bridie Cashlin's hands flew up to her ample bosom in mock horror.

"Oh Tom, and do you know John Wayne?"

"Do I know John Wayne!" And Tom's stories grew more outrageous as he told about gangsters he knew, mixing in the plots of several

films I'd seen. Then he'd lie back and laugh uproariously and wink over their heads at Eamonn and myself.

The only people he failed to make an impression on were my mother and father. They sat in a corner by themselves the whole day through. The wedding was, for them, the final disappointment. I came from a small town in county Monaghan and my father was a bank manager there. Originally he came from Galway. He was always being transferred from one part of Ireland to another because of his job. In a way he didn't really come from anywhere in the finish. The life had worn him down and, in secret, he had a taste for drink. In secret, because you'd never have known it from him. He drank in the hotel in the town with all the other professional drinkers. Drink never seemed to upset his balance. It made him increasingly silent and remorseful and he'd come home and often fall asleep, sinking into the chair until he awoke in the early hours of the morning. Then you'd hear him plod upstairs.

My mother was from the part of the country where Monaghan turns into Meath, for Monaghan and its drumlins stretch into part of that county before you see the chinks between them and the land flattens out, undulating before you beneath a sward of rich grass. My mother came from a big landowning family where the girls were given good dowries and married off, out of the way, and the boys were cloistered in the best boarding schools. We had little contact with her family when I was growing up, though I remember their big house with its orchard and their cattle belly-deep in fragrant grass.

I was an only child and all I ever wanted was to be a nurse. When I was at school and the nuns described what a vocation was I felt that that was what I had. When I mentioned it at home they thought I was talking about

Karen Ryan and Mick Connelly on their wedding day in Feakle, County Clare. Karen plays banjo, whistle and fiddle. She grew up in London and learned her music from teachers like the late Tommy Maguire. Mick comes from Bedford, north of London, and is from a well-known musical family; his father is a renowned fiddle player from Clifden, Connemara. Mick has played with Dé Danann, and has toured Germany, playing with Michael Russell and Tony McMahon. Karen and Mick are representative of that generation of fine London musicians which includes fiddle players Elaine Conwell and Teresa Heanue, box player Andy Martyn, and banjo, flute and fiddle player Johnny Carty.

Banish
Misfortune

becoming a nun—which wouldn't have been as bad in their eyes. In the end I ran away to England without telling them. It was the last year of the war and the English were crying out for nurses.

If it was tales of the lady with the lamp, thoughts of ministering to the weary and ill that drew me to nursing I was soon disabused of them; there was nothing glamorous about nursing. Men had no such ready mythology drawing them to the work they did, so they invented their own, told stories, doubled and trebled the money they were earning and the crack they were having. Women never did that, women never participated in those significant lies. Whenever I went home and was asked what nursing was like I said it was hard work, that you had better be prepared to stand for hours on feet that felt they'd been crushed, your hands raw and eyes bleary. That said, it was the first time I ever felt I belonged to anything. Women like Bridie Cashlin, who I trained with, helped each other, covered each other's mistakes, made light of the conditions we worked under—the cold wards, the regimental matrons, the overworked staff, the city around us in ruins.

I've always thought of my father's life as a bank manager as a secretive one, like his drinking. He had a position to keep up in a small town. He was one of many people,

guards and teachers among them, who lived transient lives, transplanted into parts of the country they knew little of. Whatever promise they had was somehow sapped and they could often end up permanent exiles in some backwater, forgotten about until the annual audit. I never felt that I really came from Monaghan. The girls I went to national school with all went on to secondary school in the town while I was sent to board at the St. Louis convent in another town. The girls I met there were from all over the country. Like them, I could have come from anywhere. All I have is the memory of those watery hills. At the wedding someone asked if I knew a Hughie Cailín from Monaghan. The man who asked me worked with Eamonn when he was with Murphy in the north of England. He said Hughie used to work with them, he was a grand, quiet fella. It always seemed that people, over there, thought that counties they knew little of were like small towns where everyone knew everyone else. I knew no Hughie Cailín and the fact was, even if he was from the same town as I was from, I wouldn't have known him. We would never have met. If I hadn't left Ireland I would never have married the man I did; we would never have mixed socially. Of course I couldn't say that—it would have sounded like something else altogether.

As far as my parents were concerned I was marrying below my station. My father knew well enough the type of land I was marrying into. Returning was the one condition I attached to marrying. Eamonn had land, though he never told that to many people. No man in his right mind would have worked over there if he owned enough land at home to make a living.

I was almost twenty-nine when I married. In those days that was considered old. I was a qualified nurse and midwife and was looking at spending the rest of my life in London. That said, I had no attachment to the place and I felt that I would want to raise children with space about them. Eamonn said that was what he wanted too.

As that day drew on, voices were raised in raucous argument, drink was taken, and the music never stopped—tunes dissolved into one another like the shadows of the trees outside. I could remember mart day in the town at home, when the streets would be taken over by the small farmers in from the wet hills. Each area had its own pub and they'd linger until well into the evening and beyond; their wild, wiry cattle loose in the streets, the streets deep in clabber, dealers and jobbers and men fighting while their taciturn wives waited for them to have their fill of drink. The air was charged with their voices and loud music poured from every pub doorway; those people found something in their music that vented emotions they otherwise couldn't express. But for some of the people who lived in the town it was frightening.

I could see there was something of that in the day for my mother and father. It was never as if everybody Irish liked the music anyway— even Coleen wasn't too bothered about it—there were, for many people, too many reminders of bad land and poverty in it. Maybe it had echoes for them of those fair days in the small towns; something like the skirl of pipes or the roll of drums of a besieging army drawing up outside their walls, their banners furled: something they would have pulled their curtains and barricaded their windows against.

There was plenty of fear in that room in other ways. Men, like the man I was marrying, who knew the fear and mistrust their accents inspired all over the country. Our own, my friends principal among them, who feared the Connemara men—who said I might as well be marrying into them—who feared them because they spoke a different language to us and they might be talking about us. And most of us there who were suspicious of the English, didn't like them, even if that was what our children were becoming.

When he led me out in the first dance I turned to him and said, "You're not changing your mind now, are you?" "No," he said. But I knew he must be feeling fear within him. He had all his friends drawn so closely about him, people he would have to turn away from if he was to return to Ireland. "Are you not playing?" I asked. "I will later," he said. "I have the fiddle here with me." It was, in its way, a silly question to ask, as if he would ever be without the music—but even then I had no idea of the extent to which the music defined his life. He could never get away from it.

I had a fair idea of the kind of life I was marrying into, and still it would come like a revelation to me. I could hardly tell the difference between a reel and a jig then. Some people say it all sounds the same anyway. Well, it never did all sound the same for me. I knew there were sad notes among the happy ones. That was why I always loved "The Morning Star" and I could see he was reaching somewhere within him when he played "My Love Is in America," a tune that most people played jauntily. In other

Seán Rowan from Cavan and Mick O'Grady from Kilmovee, County Mayo. Mick usually played with Dermot Grogan, from the same parish— Grogan's flute or box and Mick's fiddle. They'd talk of the well-known players Peter Horan and Fred Finn, and of Roger Sherlock, Séamus Tansey and Matt Molloy, and when Dermot drifted off to get his box from the kitchen behind the bar, O'Grady would say, "Sure, Grogan's as good as any of them." And you'd fall to thinking that the work was a distraction from the music. Then Dermot would come back and ask Mick to sing. "Ah no, I'll not" would be the reply, though with some encouragement he might, or if you were really lucky, as we were once, they might sing a duet—for the first time, faultlessly, silencing all the chatter in the early hours of the morning. "O'Grady's a good one."

Banish
Misfortune

tunes—in "The Bucks of Oranmore," for one—there was pure drive and exhilaration, and, no matter how inwardly the music was played, at some point it turned wild again and I would look at him and at the musicians playing with him and they'd be like children let loose in snow for the first time.

I asked him once did he have bad dreams. He said he had only one. The same one time and again. "I always have the one dream," he said. "I'm playing fullback in a hurling match. Although I can see no other players in it, nor a crowd either, I know it's an important game, a county final, maybe. I rise, out of what feels like a melee of men, towards the ball, coming fast at me. And, as I jump I know that I will never reach that ball. I am afraid in my bones. I want to bolt from under it. I can hear the snap of ash about me, flailing at thin air. I make to cover my head. I always wake up then. The spit dries up in my mouth. The sheets are soaked in sweat, rutted up about me."

It was on our wedding day that his worst dream came to pass—the worst because he couldn't have dreamt it. For the first time it was as if the blood in his hands had begun to solidify. What he had done to them over the years of work came on him all at once.

When he did go up to play he played "My Love Is in America" and then "Banish

Misfortune," just for luck, he said. Then he asked the other musicians to join him on the stage for "The Foxhunter's." At that stage the stiffness had begun to settle deep into the joints of his fingers. It wasn't as if he couldn't carry a tune. But it meant he would always be towed in the wake of other musicians. He could never again play the music he heard in his head. There were notes that were like rainbows he would never reach.

Of course it was years later before I found out it all started on that day, and that happened by accident—almost. RTE radio asked him to record for them and he refused. The producer, a young musician of some note, tried to change his mind, saying he had great style, the old style of playing. "But sure I have no choice," Eamonn said. "It'll only come out the one way." And then he told me about his hands, and went on to tell of the American wake and why that tune "My Love Is in America" meant so much to him. It was always there, like a splinter of memory beneath the skin. Unable to root it out.

In the evening of our wedding I left him with his brother and Coleen and went back to the hotel where my parents were staying to spend an hour with them. Eamonn was going to tell Coleen he was leaving London. I knew Coleen wouldn't believe him and might even try to change his mind and I was glad Tom was there. Tom was worried about the land. He had flown from New

York to Shannon on his way to London. "The old place is falling down," he said, "and the land badly tended. It's a great pity seeing all the work the old man put into it. All that strife over a few acres and we're throwing it away. It's no use to me, Eamonn. My life is over there. It's your place. It's in your blood."

"Land is finished," Coleen said. "Over here a man knows what he has at the end of the week."

"It's not that simple," Tom said. "Times are changing even over there." He went on to tell them about the appearance of the Tulla Band in Carnegie Hall. "Who'd have ever thought you'd see your neighbors and the children of your neighbors on the stage in a place like that? They were playing on the same bill as Pat Boone, and the lads didn't know who Pat Boone was. Some of them went out for a walk and missed their first set. The crowd went mad for them. Imagine, fourteen hours in a plane to get there and the same back. It was the first time any of us had known musicians to cross the Atlantic just to appear in America. To cross the Atlantic and still come back. They were feted in New York and Chicago. In Carnegie Hall that night they were the only band that could have played if the electricity had gone out."

"Maybe," Coleen said, "there's something in the music after all."

Eamonn used to say that Tom, if he could, would have moved the Tulla Band over there, lock, stock and drum. Tom could talk about the 1947 All Ireland football final that was played in the Polo Grounds, New York, between Cavan and Kerry as if it happened the weekend before. There was no other world for him. But we had seen the Tulla Band ourselves in the Galtymore in Crickle-wood, seen the effect they had on people, watched the people streaming towards the stage in tears, not room enough in the dance hall for a fiddler to draw back his elbow, never mind for sets.

By the time I got back from my parents' hotel they'd worn dark stains on the bar with their glasses. Another crowd of musicians were in full spate although most of the guests had gone home.

"Good luck to you, going back there," Coleen said to me, gripping my hand as tightly as he could. "You've made a great job of this fella already."

The music was stopped to allow Coleen to sing. He still kept a hold of my hand, so tightly that I winced, afraid to interrupt him as he sang, and he wound it as if it were a handle on a windlass, his voice clanking like an anchor chain emerging from the depths or like the door in a boardinghouse room creaking shut behind you.

Beating Snow Off a Rope

If you ever go over the old path to the townland of Poulacapple, on the Burren, you'll see imprinted on the rocks there the hoofmarks of "An Clas Gaibhneach"—the legendary cow whose unyielding supply of milk could fill any vessel, until someone tried to milk her into a sieve and she finally died, of exhaustion. Well, we never had any beasts like that, though we did well enough.

We moved back to Altandown in '59 and Francie, the first of three, was born in 1960. The first thing Eamonn did was to take me round his neighbors' houses. The countryside seemed to be in hibernation; there were more empty houses than houses with people in them. Talty's was the last house we called to that night. Eamonn always spoke of old Mick as if he was vital with life, but we found him old and feeble. He was expecting us, as everyone knew we were back, and when Eamonn asked him for his fire he laughed. "I never took you to be a man to hold with the old piseo," he said. And we walked back across the fields with the smouldering sod. It wasn't sentiment with Eamonn, or fear either. Whatever it was wasn't clear. I suppose he could no more not have done it than he could have walked past a house where there was music playing.

He never had much sentiment in him over anything. I could never believe the drive he had in him to work. The house didn't even have a proper roof, or running water, and we were still living in the two rooms when he bought the machinery. Rooms would be added on in the years ahead. People would say he was farsighted, but hadn't he seen it all before—it was like work was never right for him unless there was noise attached. He always had machinery in the back of his mind. He'd seen the diggers and graders gouging great lumps out of the English landscape, like dinosaurs cleaving the countryside in half. So he bought the tractor, a mowing bar and a rig to bring hay in from the fields. He contracted out all over the country—the day of the meitheal, of everyone helping everyone else, was over. The only place for the scythe now was in fields like our own, wet and neglected after years in conacre, or in fields too steep for a tractor to gain purchase in, or too small to turn in. Fields were getting bigger and marginal land was falling into disuse.

I used to think of the west of Ireland as a wide open place, facing the shifting Atlantic—that was how I pictured it in my head. Yet where I was living was similar to where I came from, the same drumlins piled up on top of each other. What eventually rooted me there was the children. Before they started school I knew few people and it would be a long time before I felt I belonged there. A long hard time in which I hardly saw my husband any other way than exhausted at night. He gave years like that; his hands stiffened about the steering wheel of the tractor, out at all hours of the day or night with a sick or ailing beast, feeling the rain on his face or the sun on the back of his neck, driving cattle across the country, watching the pall of mist from their breaths hover over them in the cold morning. All the while adding acres here and there until he trebled what he started with. And for who or for what, I'd ask him. None of our children had any interest in it. It was like the work was a force within him, a craving, a need he couldn't put a name to, something he felt in his shoulders and back, that existed for its own sake. As if the land was something that would be there for them—like the music.

He always needed something to drive him. He stopped the heavy drinking the day he got out of that hole in London, as much, knowing him, to see what it would be like as anything else. He used to say that he stopped because all he was doing was drinking to try and bring back the memories of great nights he'd had drinking and playing music and that when he did he felt like an old machine that the bits were falling from. I never knew him when he was like that— when alcohol had its own logic. I suppose I was glad enough of that.

But he never swore off it. He drank the day we got married and plenty since. The good nights came by themselves. It wasn't like that with the music. He could never get the measure of it and once his hands were gone there was nothing he could do to get those nights back.

He always had a reason to be out. I would see him in the kitchen, eyeing me furtively with the children, as if there was something between us he couldn't understand, something more than milk and solace passing between us. Sometimes I could get him to open up and he'd talk about his own mother and the music she had and I'd fall to thinking that the only memories he'd have of his children growing up would be like the fragmented memories he had of her and her music.

"Take them down into the room there,

Eamonn, and teach them," I'd say. "When I met you you were music-mad and now look at you. Go on down to Dennihey's, even—if you won't take the fiddle with you there's music there." "I'll not bother," he'd say. "They're way too fast. It's all reels now. Sure I'd swear I haven't heard a hornpipe since the 'fifties—the 'forties, even."

Just as the playing of music isn't given to everyone, neither is the teaching of it. Neither Ann nor young Tom had the interest and it was hard work for him. I wouldn't let it go though. When I was growing up we had a piano in the house and I progressed through the grades. Though I had no genuine interest in it the music came easily enough to me, the notes tinkling like water through the house. I suppose, in some ideal world, people would have congregated about a piano and sung the gentle melodies of Thomas Moore. I didn't know why it seemed important to me; perhaps it was all that we had. I got Eamonn to show me the fingering on the tin whistle and a couple of simple tunes and I taught the children myself. Then I'd push him, time and time again, into playing with them. Sometimes you'd think all that was in the house was music. "Ye'll have your own céilí band yet," Joe Considine would say, passing on the road, and his children would come up to the house too. I bought a record player and the new records—Joe Burke, Seán Maguire and Roger

Sherlock—as they came out, and I played them constantly. He'd be below in the room with them, Ann and Tom out of tune, unable to keep time, unable to concentrate.

The music could never be driven away. Dam it up in one place and it seeps through in another. Ignore it altogether and find your foot keeping time anyway. Drive it underground and it bubbles up like a turlough on the Burren. It broke through in Francie. I think Eamonn could see himself in him. "All I'm doing is passing on where the notes are," he said. It was enough. Francie lived for music from the start.

I'd watch them through the open door, Eamonn talking about tunes like the old man he used to tell of himself. Not like that, like this. The music was a creaking floor board in his head. He'd take up the fiddle and for a while the music would sweep from him. Then the stiffening would start again and you could see it in his face. He'd put it down. "Eamonn, that was great," I'd say. "Wasn't it, Francie?" But he'd stalk from the room. Francie with his mouth hanging open. Later that night he'd take it up again. I'd look out into the hallway and see the shaft of light swal-

Paddy Killourhy of Ballyfaudeen, south of Doolin, an area where old traditions lasted a long time— the last native Irish speaker died recently. The Killourhys—Paddy and his brother Johnny—were immersed in music and storytelling from the start. When they were growing up the area was rich in musicians, and they learned to play in the local style.

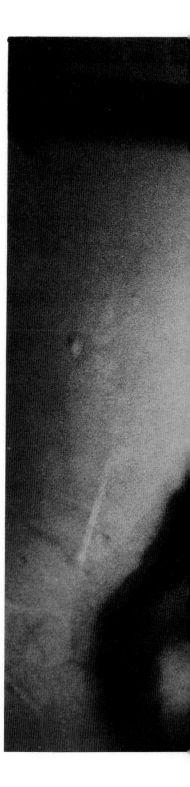

the
Heartbeat
of IRISH
MUSIC

Beating
Snow Off
a Rope

lowed up in the darkness of Francie's room. Francie listening, the door ajar, his father willing his hands to loosen up—just for the one night—just once, so he could drive the ghosts of music from him. "My Love Is in America."

Francie was winning all before him. He was at every feis and fleadh and music competition all over the country. At the start Eamonn went with him, until the day he was in competition with four other children. I was there as well. I asked Eamonn who he thought would win after they'd played their pieces. "It could be any of them," he said. "I couldn't judge it at any rate. They were all good." Francie took first place, a trophy, and medals were given to the second- and third-placed children. The fourth child got nothing. She looked as if something had been stolen from her. "There's no point in that," Eamonn said. "That's me finished with competitions if that's what it's all about. Where's the fun in it? Maybe she'll never play again." He didn't believe the music—the music by itself—held any meaning for her.

Competitions were a new idea. I couldn't see what the complaint was—if it was encouraging people to play, where was the harm in it? "No," he said. "It changes the music. What gives anyone the right to judge?"

He never watched Francie play in a competition again. I took Francie all over the country, wherever he wanted to go. If I couldn't take him someone else always could. Cars, you see, were everywhere, where, in the old days, people in the country going out for a night's music would have to walk, or at best, walk four or five miles to a crossroads and get a lift in a lorry to a dance hall or a house-dance at the back of beyond. Cars were everywhere, rushing in every direction, sometimes all in the one direction. You could get to know the whole country in a very short time where once you could only have imagined it from hearing peo-

A cloud moving over the Burren, County Clare.

ple talk about it. It would be like England or America—a place you had in your head.

Francie was going to be a musician from the start. He was good at school but he had everything pulling him in all directions. When he said he was giving it up for music we didn't know what to say. Eamonn was useless like that—he wouldn't say anything to them. "If he's like me," he said, "he'll just go and do it anyway, and anyhow, can't he always go back to school? There isn't a day's work in him anyhow." Joe Considine said that these were changed times, that a man could make a living playing music. It mightn't be great, but it was still a living. "I don't know what you're on about," Eamonn said to me. "You're the one who encouraged him."

Beating
Snow Off
a Rope

I used to think—my two daft sons, each in their separate worlds. I used to harry Eamonn to be in some way less tolerant with them—to make them work. He was out all hours and they weren't interested. Tom was going to be something different from week to week: an engineer, a soldier, a priest, an inventor. He stuck hard to his books, his head in them all the time. He was so mild-mannered Eamonn used to say that if he smoked he'd have tipped the ash into his pocket. I used to wonder if he had any drive at all in him. And Ann, following the two of them around, they ignoring her. At least she was practical and knew what she wanted. She was going to be a nurse or maybe a doctor from the day she took my bandages and wrapped the dog in them.

Francie, though, had luck you couldn't squander. He was good at whatever he turned his hand to, at school and at music, and what he wasn't good at—hurling—he was lucky at. In a small parish like ours you could wait generations to have a team win anything and, even then, there would be trouble making up the numbers—anyone near enough the right age would get a run out. That was how Francie became a substitute. Once they became old enough to hurl, Eamonn was transformed—hurling was a way of life for him. He was extravagant about hurling in a way he could

never be about music. To listen to him, the young lads of the parish were playing the best hurling seen in the country since the time of Cúchulainn. A good hurler was molded by the hands of God. Whatever went on in the molding Tom must have been touched. It was "Tom this" and "Tom that" around the house for weeks. It was something I'd have to see for myself.

I remember them coming home from matches disconsolate and beaten. I remember the start of the championship that year, the jibes in the parish—"Yis wouldn't beat snow off a rope." The momentum that gathered through the parish as they progressed, so that by the day of the final in Ennis people came down from the hills, risen from their sick beds. Mick Talty on the sideline on his walking aid, a parish jersey on under his jacket.

And it was a hard-fought affair. There was no drawing back. Round about where we lived they used to question a man's mettle by asking: "How would he be under a dropping ball?" They all stood up that day. It was the first hurling match I was ever at and Ann had to explain to me what was going on. When Tom smashed his arm into the opposing mid-fielder's chest, winding him, I couldn't believe what I was seeing. I turned to Eamonn. "He's dirty," I said. "No," he said, his face alight. "He's hard."

By halftime they were six points down. Eamonn was out on the field with Tom. He was emphasizing some point with his fists. Tom was nodding, his head down, kicking at tufts of grass. The second half started. Our lads had a slight breeze with them. Straight away they were another point behind. Then, from the puck-out, Tom fielded the ball cleanly, he feinted to his left an instant before setting off to his right. He seemed to slide to a halt, already pivoting, and unleashed all the coiled-up energy within him, then tipped back on his heels, as if knocked there by the recoil. The ball smashed over the bar from the middle of the field. The crowd erupted: "G'wan lads, tear inta them." Tom had perfect buoyancy. He hooked and blocked and scored six points, all of them from play. Four of them came from the wing, on the run, and one from where he drew on the ball in midair. I was thinking, "Is this my son?"

With only a couple of minutes left they brought on Francie. "They're desperate," Ann said. Francie looked ungainly. He shuffled more than ran onto the field. They were two points behind when Joe Considine's son James sent a long free forward. The ball was dropping into the square. Francie flung himself at it. "He won't even see it," I said to Ann. "He's half-blind without his glasses." He went up in a melee of players, flailed at it and somehow it caught the handle of his stick and trickled slowly past the wrong-footed goalkeeper.

Dennihey's bar never closed that night. There were bonfires on all the hills out of the town. Francie played music and Mick Talty, pressing down on the walking aid, lifted his feet far enough from the ground to dance a few steps. Even Eamonn played, and he laughed and joked: "Do you know this one? Do you know that one?" Him and Francie, and young Considine on the box, pumping the music out, Francie announcing his retirement from hurling in case he hurt his hands, Tom swinging the cup aloft, telling him he was soft in the head. Considine driving the box, his face contorted; flute and concertina players that were said to be dead or not playing anymore piling in from the hills. Men prophesying senior titles, All Ireland titles even, amid the fierce, wild exultation of the music. "Oh Jasus, Joe Cooley's alive again," Talty shouted. People telling me they didn't know why they were crying.

"I didn't know myself," I said to Eamonn. "Sure I'm not even from here."

"You are now," he said.

PART THREE
the eighties
and the
nineties

Johnny O'Leary, born in Gneeveguila, County Kerry, in the heart of the area known as Sliabh Luachra. The words "Sliabh Luachra" also describe the style of music usually heard in this area, on the Cork-Kerry border, and stretching into north Kerry and Limerick. It is renowned for its polkas and slides and for the vigor and infectious good humor with which it is played. Johnny O'Leary is one of the great exponents of this music, playing in the tradition of well-known players like Padraig O'Keefe, Julia Clifford, Denis Murphy, and Tom Billy. O'Leary has been widely recorded on albums such as "The Trooper."

Piseogs

Talking over the head of Brendan Begley. Brendan is a great stylist, from Dingle, the Gaeltacht of west Kerry. His family are all well-known singers and musicians.

It started with my uncle Tom coming back from America every summer and it wound up when the thaw came in Alaska—at least that's one way of making sense of it. They were all arguing in the kitchen about me going to America, as if I wasn't there. "He might never come back," my mother said. "Those days are gone," my father said. "He'll be back. Sure don't people go there every week. There's no permanence in it anymore." "It's Tom's fault," she said, "filling his head with nonsense about the States." "Won't he be better off with Tom—at least he'll be with his own," he said.

To tell the truth it started years before that. It was always there in a way, but to tell a story you have to begin somewhere. The beginning for me was in another place altogether. It was the day my father found me above in the fields at Lisnamac.

I was about ten at the time. I was out playing by myself. Tom, my brother, had his head stuck in a book, as usual. All he'd want to do was tell you the sto-

Fanore, in the north Burren, County Clare.

Piseogs

ries he read. I had to make my own fun or go looking for Frank Considine to play with. I used to go up to Lisnamac all the time. I'd hide in the trees up there. Then, that one morning, I was on my way along the pad towards them when, for some reason, I drifted from it. I went over to look at a hollow in the field. It was early in the morning and the dew was still heavy on the grass. The hollow was filled with a mist and I walked down into it. I don't know how long I was down there. I have no memory of it beyond hearing music. I didn't see anything or anyone, playing or otherwise. It just seemed the most natural thing in the world that there should be music coming from nowhere in a hollow in a field—music like I'd never heard before.

My father was driving the cattle back along the cobbled road when he saw me. I heard him telling Mick Talty after that he shouted at me several times before I answered and that I looked scared. I didn't know who he was for a minute. Then I ran towards him. "What were you doing down there?" he asked. "I was listening to the music," I told him.

He was agitated about it. As agitated as he got the time the wind came up and lifted the stooked crops out of Considine's fields and landed them over in ours. "It must have been a fairy wind," I said to him and he snapped back that there was no such thing and who the hell

was filling me with old piseogs? The day I heard the music in the hollow he took me over to Talty's place and told old Mick what had happened. Mick nodded. "There's supposed to be hungry grass in that field," he said. He said if it ever happened to me again I was to take my jacket or pullover off and put it back on inside out. That would break the hold it would have over you. Try as I might—and I went over every tuft of grass in that hollow for a long time after—I could never get it to happen again. As I say, I have no memory of it beyond hearing the music and I have no real memory of the music either other than that it was lonely.

It was after that day that I got serious about playing the fiddle and it began to take up all my time. It wasn't something I could ever explain—the feelings that came to me playing music, what I used to think of as the hidden bits of tunes, where the music would lead you astray and you'd forget about time altogether. My mother, who started me off, had nothing more to show me and I used to follow the old fella round the place. For a while it even looked as if I might be a farmer, for I'd go out and help him with his work. He knew well enough though— he must have been like me at one time himself— he knew I was only helping him in exchange for music, and he kept his part of the bargain.

I could never see what his problem was

with his hands. They were splayed flatter than they should have been and the knuckles were like a fighter's, covered in scar tissue, but he was a mighty player and all I ever wanted was to be as good as him. Sometimes, with him, it was like he couldn't get the sounds he was after and he'd put down the fiddle and walk out of the house. Later, at night, I'd hear him at it again. I used to always leave the door on the bedroom ajar so I could be listening to what was going on in the kitchen, if anyone came what my mother called "céilí-ing," visiting. I used to lie in the bed and his music would run before me in colors—red for sadness and yellow if he was happy. He would be like a pot simmering with music.

People would come round and they would talk about the old days. The old days always were a lot more interesting to me than the times we were living in. I could hear my father going on about the stories the man who taught him to play used to tell. About the piper who was blind and who had a black dog following him everywhere. He could see the dog himself even though he could see nothing else.

When old Talty got the stye on his eye he asked me up to the house. He told me he had the cure for it but it wouldn't work on himself. I plucked the thorns of the whitethorn bush, blessed them and threw them back across my shoulder, saying some prayer for three Mondays

after the other, and the stye went. He gave me the cures for different things—a sprained ankle and the bad heart. He said they were mine by right, that they came down through my grandmother's people. I only ever half practiced them, and people, noting my lack of enthusiasm, soon stopped coming up to the house looking for me.

Whether it was over that day in the hollow or not, or was from my own devising, I spent a lot of time in some badly-lit world where the shadow of one thing could take on the form of another. I would be on my bicycle. I would be returning from the town to Altandown in a freezing fog—the four miles and all of it uphill. The lights on the bicycle wouldn't penetrate the fog. Every so often somebody would hurtle out of the gloom past me, going downhill. Sometimes they muttered something indecipherable. Then they were gone and all that was left of them was the music of the bicycle spokes whirring into the mist. I could never make them out. It might have been a Considine or one of the Hayes's or Joe Mac's. They might have been one of the ghosts that were said to have haunted that stretch of road. I would get off the bicycle and begin to push it uphill, feeling the fog clammy against my skin. Afraid to look round for fear there was a black dog behind me. Even though I had a way with dogs, I knew this one wouldn't like me.

They'd talk about old musicians they knew as well as the ones they'd heard about. About Doran and Cooley and Tom Power. There was never a piper like Doran, my father would say, and then they'd talk about Saco. I could nearly see Saco better than any of them, even though I knew the music of Cooley and Doran from records and had never heard him play. His right name was Jacko Downes. He was from down round Kilrush, but he spent all his time between our place and Flagmount. They used to say he was a priest or a Christian Brother at one time. Anyhow, he fell out with God and joined the rest of us in the divil's army. He played the concertina or melodion. I heard my father and Mick Talty discussing him many times. "It was in Taltys' kitchen," my father would say, "I first heard him play 'Saco's Jig.'"

Saco was a ventriloquist. You could be in the room and he'd have someone call you out and there'd be no one there. He had umpteen different tricks in cards. You could be playing with him and all the good

Danny Foley, Peter Mackey, Bernie Whelan and Josephine Marsh in Friel's of Miltown Malbay during Willie Clancy week. In its purest form the seisiún is a communal gathering for pooling ideas, learning new music— an outpouring of technique and, far more importantly, of emotion. It draws on the emotions of those enfolded to achieve a kind of timelessness. There are no limits on the number of people who can participate and time itself ceases to be a factor. In Ireland a good seisiún will be spoken of again and again. It achieves a legendary and near mythological status.

cards would come circling back to him, or he'd wind up with a fistful of cards he could hardly hold. He would read your fortune in the cards; he'd let on he had to put an extra glass on over his glasses to give him the second sight.

"You know the way he could imitate the sounds of instruments?" Mick said. "Do you remember the time he was working in Ennis for the big contractor and the man put him digging trenches? It was all pick and shovel work—no compressors in those days. Anyhow, Saco was a good enough worker, but he would be a distraction on any job he was on— voices shouting at you from all angles. That was why he was put working on his own. Well, there was a flute player on that job and when he heard that Saco played the concertina, he asked him to bring it to work the next day. Saco brought his concertina and the two of them went at it, playing different bouts of music between them in the break. Well the whistle went to go back to work and Saco was still playing. "Put down that concertina," the foreman says to him,

Piseogs

"and get back down that trench." Saco did as he was told; he hopped back down into the drain, leaving the concertina behind him on the bank. The poor foreman stood on the bank, the face on him like a melted candle, looking down at Saco shoveling and the reel finishing itself on the concertina behind his back! That was as much as he could handle and poor Saco got his marching papers, but it didn't matter much to him, I suppose."

I used to ask my father about Mick Talty. Why was he always in our house? Had he no family of his own? They're all gone, he'd say, they all went to America and only for Mick Talty there'd be no music in this house. Only for the likes of Mick Talty there'd be no music in the country.

It would only be when there was no one else in the house—when my mother was gone to bed—that my father would turn to play the music. I suppose he knew hundreds of tunes but he'd only play the same ones over and over. When I got older I fell into the fashion of knowing a lot of music and it took me a while to discover what he was at. I thought he was boring. I couldn't see what he saw in that handful of tunes: "The Bucks," "My Love Is in America," "Rakish Paddy," "The Sailor's Bonnet," "The Wheels of the World," "The Brown Coffin," "The Priest and his Boots," "Morrison's," "The Kesh,"

"Saco's" and "The Foxhunter's."

Then he had a tune of his own he would turn to. If all those tunes were to stay in my head forever, then that one tune was to haunt me, for he had no ending for it. Sometimes he'd just phrase and rephrase the first few bars, other times he'd turn it, looking for an ending; sometimes it was a reel and sometimes he exaggerated it into a hornpipe, and other times still he'd play it like an air. I could never see why he couldn't finish it, but in his playing there was something that scared me.

It reminded me of a story they used to tell about a bailiff called McFadyean. He was sent down from the north of the country in the bad times past. He tormented the people and he was cursed by an old woman for it. It was said that when he died rats crawled along the rafters and down the walls towards his coffin. Men beat them back with spades and sleáns—not out of respect but from some notion they had that funerals were inviolable. I could see them— shrieking in the darkness when my father played that part of an air—huge black, cadaverous rats, their sides bent together with the hunger. Even then McFadyean got no respect, as a priest turned back his coffin from the gates of the church, denying him burial. It was said that he walked for eternity along the apex of the graveyard wall on hot needles, unable to get in.

It was said that his coffin had seeped corruption; that those who carried it bore scars where it had cut into their shoulders, marking them for life, that they stumbled and fell beneath it. It was said that none of this was true, that he'd fallen ill and was buried quickly, tearing at the lid of the closed coffin.

When I went to America I knew more about America from television than anyone from any other generation. It was easy to blame Tom. He was home every summer after the summer he first took his wife back. Every year he rented a house in Miltown Malbay for the Willie Clancy Week. He was a great man to talk. My father said he should have been a politician. But he wasn't making America any more real for me. I saw it every week. My father used to talk about the first time he saw the John Ford western *Stagecoach* in the cinema. Before that he thought America was all cities. He never heard about people who went anywhere else and he couldn't believe the size of Monument Valley, dwarfing the stagecoach. Whatever else about him, and I used to argue with him all the time about music, he never stood in our way.

My mother was worried though. Before I went I was going out with a girl from the North. She was a fiddle player and a great singer, but she was a few years older than me. "She's only after a man," my mother would say. "She's

clever. They all are up that way." I'd say, "Like yourself is it? Sure that's where you're from." She'd always ignore you if she didn't like what you were saying. Then, when I broke up with that girl and was heading to America a few months later, she said, "It's a pity you didn't stick with that woman. Marriage might have been the making of you."

It was hardly like the times of the American wakes they used to talk about. If I wanted I could come back the next week. Indeed, there were plenty of people who prophesied that I would. The year we won the county minor Ownie Daly had told us we wouldn't beat snow off a rope; now he told me, the day before I left, that I'd be back soon enough for my mother's brown bread.

It was just that I had to see for myself. I wanted to know if the place was real or if it was just like the stories of times past—though a confection of the television and cinema—that exceeded the possibilities of real life.

Piseogs

The Roaring Twenties

"Will you turn that fucking thing off," I shouted at the barman. He was perfectly reasonable: "Mr. Callaghan says the machines stay on all the time. The customers like the machines," he said. "Even the fucking talking ones?" "Even the talking ones." He went on polishing a glass with the tails of his shirt.

I walked back over to the stage. The carpet was sticking to the soles of my feet. "Do you

Jim Cerrigan from Callan, County Kilkenny. The southeast of Ireland was an area noted for its pipers in the last century and the early part of this one—the Cashs, Rowsomes and Dorans from Wexford—and O'Neill in his Irish Minstrels and Musicians *writes of James Byrne, a travelling piper who settled near Mooncoyne in Kilkenny, and of Adam Tobin from the same area. Jim comes from a family of musicians. He now lives in Ennis.*

know 'The Kilfenora Jig'?" I asked Bernadette. She stared at me blankly and shook her head. "Do you know any jig?" I asked.

Give us 'Danny Boy,'" a voice shouted from the darkness.

Tom had a nice place up in the Catskills. He wasn't involved in the business much anymore. If he could have he'd have pulled the pin on it long ago, at least that was what he told me. He wanted out, he wanted to return home. Hannah, his wife, was the only thing standing in his way. The first time he brought Hannah home she hated the place. It was so damp—rained all the three weeks. She took to my mother and father's bed and didn't get out of it. The year he brought her home was the start of him coming back every year. Before that he'd holidayed in Las Vegas. Tom liked to gamble but he played the percentages—he could afford to lose as easily as he could stand winning. He always gambled small stakes.

Hannah was a divorcee. He was afraid what people would say about her. "I don't know what you're worried about," my father told him. "If they say anything at all you'll not be here to listen to it." That was when he brought her home for the first time.

"Did you bring me the praying hands?" she asked me when I arrived at the house. I took the effigy of two hands joined in prayer, a rosary beads entwined between them, from my bag. The house was cluttered with Irish religious imagery—a statue of Our Lady of Knock, rosary beads from Lough Derg in a glass case, The Child of Prague, even the picture of Pope Paul VI flanked by the two dead Kennedys that you hardly ever saw at home anymore. "Goddam it," Tom said, "she ain't even a Catholic."

Still, there were no relics in Tom's study where we sat drinking fifty-year-old malt whiskey the night I arrived. No religious ones at any rate. There were certificates from The Knights of Columbus, thanking him for his charitable contributions, pictures of him with Mayor Daley of Chicago, with various New York mayors and sporting celebrities, with one of the Kennedys and, in pride of place, a shot of himself with de Valera on an airport tarmac. He even had a photograph taken on the stage in Carnegie Hall. He was standing with his arm draped around P. J. Hayes's shoulder the night the Tulla Band played there.

"What I need to know," he said, "is if you're coming into the business. I could use a smart head now I'm getting out. I hadda take on a partner and shut my eyes to what he's taking under the table."

"I don't see myself in the bar business, Tom," I said. "I'd just be happy to make the few bob playing music."

"Well, think about it," he said, and I knew he was disappointed. "It's there for you. I'll talk to Callaghan—my partner—an' see what he comes up with."

It was Callaghan who landed me in the Bowery Maid. I walked past it twice before I knew it was there and even then, if it hadn't been for the leprechaun, I wouldn't have found it. "Best Irish bar in Noo Yawk," the "leprechaun" shouted, shoving himself into my path. I was lost. Nobody I asked had a clue what I was talking about. I crossed the street to avoid the leprechaun who was giving out fliers. Then I had to come back up past him again. "I'm looking for the Bowery Maid," I told him. "Isn't that what I'm trying to tell you, guy—best Irish bar in Noo Yawk—say, you from the old country?"

The Bowery Maid had hardly any street frontage, yet it was cavernous inside. It was awful cold and stank of stale beer and had hardly any natural light. When it was built it was built for functional reasons—to throw out as much drink as fast as possible. Its halcyon days were long past. Your eyes were drawn to the stage over which there was a huge banner: IF YOU'RE IRISH COME INTO THE PARLOR. Below that there was a painting, stained with nicotine, of what might have been the Great Blasket island, floating like the edge of an up-turned tire in a greasy sea. Plastic leprechauns and shamrocks dangled from the ceiling.

Callaghan, who I never met, told me over the phone to ask for the manager. Bat Connors was his name, though he preferred to be known as T-Bone Connors, on account of his love of red meat. He was a Kerryman and appeared surprised to see me. "Nobody tells me nothing," he said. "So you're related to Tommy?" He was surprised that Tommy had sent me there. The worst

bar he owned. I explained that he had nothing to do with it. He left it to Callaghan. "That horseshit," he said. "He leaves everything to Callaghan now. Callaghan doesn't give a damn about this place. It's all just real estate to him. Thinks he's Elvis in that pink cadillac of his."

"Can you play that thing?" he asked, pointing at the fiddle case. "I'm handy enough," I told him. "Well," he said, "you'll have your work cut out here because I can't get rid of Bernadette. She came with the place and the customers love her. I reckon Bernadette was the piano player who fucked up all those Coleman recordings. She's old enough anyhow. I must ask her and see if she remembers, that's if she can remember anything."

For the few weeks I spent there I got on well with Connors. He liked the music himself and remembered the good times when some of the greatest musicians there were played all over New York. He was fond of Johnny Cronin from his own part of the country and every time I'd come into the bar he'd shout like Cronin used to: "If I had the wings of a sparrow, the dirty great arse of a crow, I'd fly to the top of the steeple and shit on the people below."

Bernadette was a different matter altogether. She did look old enough to have played with Coleman. "She used to be all right till she got that new contraption," Connors said. She

had a synthesizer with a built-in drumming machine, which she usually played so that it sounded like a church organ. So, as well as having to contend with her out-of-key organ, I could expect a drummer to join in unexpectedly—an invisible one who could wind up playing a waltz or a samba, even as I played a reel.

Tom had the finest collection of 78s I ever saw, and Connors, who may not have witnessed it but talked like he had, could fill your head with musical history. The music had been so popular in the 'twenties that everyone got to record. The standard was uneven, to say the least. On one legendary recording of the piper Liam Walsh, the fiddle player with him was well into the second part of the tune before Walsh had finished the first. Then the piano was added to everything just to pick out the steps for dancing classes—this was a market in itself. You had out-of-tune pianos pulsing behind or in front of the music. It never seemed to bother the record companies that the accompanist wouldn't have learned their part. Though, to be fair, there were good ones like Whitey Andrews, a Welshman, who backed Coleman on some recordings.

Bernadette could definitely have made a good living in those days. She couldn't see where one tune differed from another. It would

Playing at the fair in Spancilhill, County Clare.

have been better if her machine had a reel or a jig program on it. I was never even sure that she was Irish. Any time I questioned her she managed to answer in monosyllables or speak so low I couldn't make out what she was saying. She had, though, perfected the right type of singing voice for her choice of material. Her hands hovered above the keyboard and her head moved in jerky motions, in time with the music. It was like she was on strings attached to the ceiling. Every night she sang the same songs: " A Mother's Love," "Danny Boy," " If We Only Had Old Ireland," all the usual ones—all the ones the customers wanted. If she wasn't too hot on jigs and reels, neither were the customers.

For the time I was there I played five nights a week. On my nights off I would go trawling the bars, looking for music. I started to play with an Armagh fiddle player named Caulfield. It didn't last long. He was on his way back to Ireland. Caulfield was a great man to argue music. He would disagree with you for the sake of it. Because his style was northern I thought I was on safe ground saying that Tommy Peoples was the best fiddle player. "A great player, that's for sure, but there's no one to touch Seán Maguire." That was even though he sounded nothing like Maguire himself. He was a good, vigorous player and time spent with him would keep you on your toes. I thought I had him one night. "Doran," I said, "there's no one to touch him." "Rooney," he said, "Rooney from Cross." "Cross?" I said. "Crossmaglen." Well, I had heard of Crossmaglen but I had never heard of Rooney.

"He learned from Felix Doran, Johnny's brother," Caulfield said, "and he's married to his daughter. Boy, he's some piper. He can tear the arse out of any tune." But I could never be a hundred percent sure with Caulfield, sure that he wasn't inventing someone to put an end to an argument.

It was from Caulfield that I got the contacts for the job, and that was how I met Kolinsky or Maguire, or whatever he called himself.

They were gutting out the old brownstone houses, turning them into warrens of apartments. It was hard, dirty work. The walls and ceilings we were pulling down had a century's dust and soot in them. After I got home and washed I'd have to wash again, and again. The soot seeped back out of my pores; it

Nicky McAuliffe, Geraldine Cotter, Anne McAuliffe, Bríd Donoghue, Nick Adams. A whistle and flute seisiún in Queally's, Miltown Malbay, during Willie Clancy week. Willie Clancy was one of the greatest of pipers and a native of Miltown Malbay, where, in July every year, a summer school is held in his honor. Musicians travel from all over Ireland and from abroad to listen to lectures, attend workshops, and, above all else, play music. The workshops are taught by some of the best musicians within the tradition, people like Bobby Casey and Martin Hayes on fiddle, and Eamonn Cotter on flute.

formed a film on my skin like grease.

Kolinsky came onto the job one day. He was selling carpets and Canadian Army surplus boots out of the back of a van. I got talking to him. "I'm part Irish myself," he told me. "One of my people was a Maguire from a place called Kilmallock." Kolinsky had a face on him you'd expect to see on a man carrying a sack of rubbish down the steps of one of the brownstones. The sack would contain ancient plaster made from horsehair and the timber laths that were nailed to the stud partitions it came from. Kolinsky looked as if bits of the laths with nails attached were permanently sticking through the bag and into his back. And his skin had a smoky grey look to it. He looked martyred.

Kolinsky was a man who was always doing something while he was waiting on something else to come up. I met him for a drink that night. He asked me what I did. "Didn't you see me?" I said.

"Come on man," he said. "Nobody does that for a living." I told him I played music.

"I have interests in the music business," he said. "I could be your agent. Everybody with talent needs an agent in this town. Are you any good?"

"Agent. How much?"

"Twenty-five percent."

"Ten," I said.

"Fifteen."

"Fifteen then," I agreed. "Fifteen percent of nothing is still nothing."

Kolinsky was managing a rock band called The Cropdusters. That was when my life got taken over and I lost the job which, bad and all as it was, still fed me. The band were successful enough; they had a cult following, and played different types of music, mixing them together. It was a hazardous living. The money I made I spent on drink and other bad habits. We played at everything from gallery openings—where people stood around as if they had something simmering in their bowels and were afraid to confide in one another—to concerts.

We threshed like an engine turning in on itself—powering nothing. The music reached a crescendo so fast it felt as if individual parts of

Irene Martin, Tim Dennihey, Mary Friel and Willie Keane dance a set in Gleason's of Coor, in west Clare. Irene and Mary teach dancing at the fabled Brooks' Academy in Dublin. Willie Keane is one of the great exponents of the west Clare set, and Tim Dennihey, as well as dancing, broadcasts a music program on Clare FM. A native of Cahirciveen, County Kerry, he is a noted singer, and has released two fine albums, "A Winter's Tear" and "A Thimbleful of Song."

the machine were shaking loose—notes colliding—igniting—the throb of the bass guitar, demented drumming, the harmonica honking, the singer's voice caught in an emotional trough.

"Ladies and Gentlemen—on lead violin . . . " All of it threatening to overwhelm me, the electricity humming through me as I stepped forward into the heat and changing colors of the spotlight. The dance floor undulating—hands stretched out towards me—bodies wavering like a sward of grass before the wind. The barest minimum of air rustling through the saxophone. My notes disappearing like spumes of breath of a cold morning, spiraling into nothing, their life that brief.

The oddments of music I was playing were like cast-offs or junk that you'd throw into a cupboard and forget about. But Kolinsky talked big, big percentages, big record deals and I was easily seduced.

All I could think of was fast playing. So fast you couldn't hear half the notes, at least I was the only person who could. Even if they weren't there I could still hear them, or the shades of them anyway. I went home that sum-

mer for the first time. I hadn't a visa to work in the States. I was an illegal and that was my own fault. I should have stuck with Tom until my papers came through. Even if I'd gone up into the Catskills he'd have fixed me up with something. As it was I was worried I mightn't get back in. I should have been worried about how they'd take me at home.

My reappearance worried my mother. I had a head of long hair, down my back. I was spaced-out most of the time and playing the fast music that few people liked. Reels—always reels—only reels. My sister called me the rock star. My brother said I was a wanker.

I couldn't wait to get back. I got my hair cut and flew to the States through London. It was cheaper and I was told that Immigration paid less attention to what came in from Heathrow. I had headed notepaper from a New York GAA club and I got my sister to type me out a letter inviting me over to lecture on Irish music and teach dancing. She thought that

Paddy Canny, Maghera, one of the great east Clare stylists. Along with his brother-in-law P. J. Hayes, Peadar O'Loughlin on flute and Bridie Lafferty on piano, he recorded an album, "All Ireland Champions—Violin," in the early 'sixties that was the first of its kind, the first modern album of Irish music. Unfortunately, this album is hard to come by, despite continuing rumors of its impending reissue. At that time Canny was widely recorded for radio and television; his version of the tune "The Job of Journeywork," used as the signature tune for the radio program of the same name, is the standard version. From one decade to another musicians appear to pass in and out of fashion, but Paddy Canny is still playing great music.

was a nice touch. Me with the two left feet.

I got back in. I was hungover most of the time now. I gave up my apartment and ended up sleeping on different people's floors. I was staying with a man named Guilfoyle, a New York-born box player. There was a market for music down in the Bronx he told me—anyone who could keep time could get on the circuit, playing for feiseanna and dance competitions. The band wasn't pulling in enough money and, when Guilfoyle suggested it, I was agreeable to giving it a go. The only problem was that all the competitions started in the mornings when my hangovers would be worst.

The first morning Guilfoyle dragged me from the couch. "Come on, man. We're late," he said. We took a cab. The driver was an Armenian who spoke little English and got lost on the way. Guilfoyle had as bad a head as I had. The piano player, a veteran of the circuit, was disgusted; it was his living. "You two better go off

and get the cure," he said, "but go one at a time. You'll both want to be on stage by lunch—that's when it gets serious." We didn't have to be told twice. Guilfoyle went first—half an hour each, we agreed.

In the middle of the first set a spider landed on the bridge of my fiddle. I was terrified of spiders. I shook it loose and it pinged up in the air, hanging there on a thread of gossamer before my face. I was near the turn of the tune. I bowed frantically and blew on it. All that did was to set it in motion, swaying on its thread—the motion carrying it closer and closer to my face. I tilted the chair backwards. As it grew nearer I hooked my heels on the side of the piano and pushed farther back, until the chair was balanced precariously and could go no farther. My head was pounding and threads of sweat were running through my hair and down my face. There was salt burning my eyes and my mouth was dry. I played faster and faster. I could barely make out the shapes of the dancers—seven- and eight-year-olds—but I could see they'd given up trying to dance the figure. They were roaring and shouting and slam-dancing as their teachers tried to pull them apart.

New York, Guilfoyle told me, was full of spiders. What I had was a recognized condition. I should talk to someone about it.

I metamorphosed in the afternoon—back to normal—and I got three hundred dollars for that gig and there was more where it came from. Somehow Kolinsky found out about it and demanded his cut. "Lenny," I said, "I don't mind fifteen percent of what you hustle up but not of what I hustle for myself." "It's the principle," he said. "Everybody else pays twenty percent." That was true, but I still didn't pay him.

In the Roaring Twenties pub I met an Aran Islander. We took to drinking together all the time. He played with me from time to time, and I managed to get him on stage with the band. He was a much better percussionist than the drummer we had. He could make the bodhrán sound like the wind brushing the froth of waves, or like thunder, or, in discordant time, like the hooves of fatigued horses drawing near the finishing post.

In other ways he was an eccentric. He believed that the continual translation of songs and poetry from Irish to English was eroding his native language. That was how we wound up in the recording studio. He had translated a song into Irish—"Tá sé go léir Thart Anois, a Leanbh Gorm," a Bob Dylan song "It's All Over Now, Baby Blue"—and he asked me to play on the recording.

It was a Sunday afternoon when we entered the studio. There were the two of us, a Puerto Rican snare-drummer and two crates of beer. The studio was in the Bronx, built hard up against the El. Every time a train passed the whole place rattled. Whether the Inis Oír man knew this beforehand I never found out. He made the most of it, mixing the sound of the on-rushing train onto the track—so, as the song drew to a finish and his voice caught in a sean nós pitch: Tá sé. Tá sé. Tá sé . . . the train whooshed, the beer bottles rattled and the snare-drum shook, all by itself. My fiddle screaming behind it all.

Kolinsky heard about that too. He came looking for money even though there was none involved—it was a favor. "There ain't no favors in showbusiness," he said. What I used to admire in him—his energy, like electricity fizzing between the pylons, and his way of talking, like dry snow crunching underfoot—had begun to repel me. He seemed to grow increasingly stri-dent, inhabiting a dimly lit, half-fermented world where nothing ever got finished, skim-ming like a stone across the surface of water while I waited on him to plop. "What's happen-ing with the band recording?" I asked.

"Why don't you go out and hustle?" he shouted.

I was still sleeping on Guilfoyle's couch when there came a knock at the door one Monday night. I looked out through the fish eye and saw a baroque figure, with a long black coat and black-brimmed hat, ringlets dangling beneath it. I was about to go back to what I had been doing when it struck me that Orthodox Jews didn't go out looking for converts, as far as I knew anyway. Besides, there was something familiar about the stance of the figure beyond the door. I opened it and the man outside pushed past me into the room. He took off the hat and the ringlets came away with it. "Jesus Christ, what are you at, Kolinsky? You're not even Jewish."

"I'm part Jewish," he said. "Nobody asks to see down your trousers, you know. I'm in trouble, man. I'm gonna get my legs broken. I've been followed all day. You should see these two guys—Stone Age man or what!" He was looking to borrow money.

"Where will you go?" I asked.

"Alaska," he said. "My brother has bought a bar up there; he wants me to manage it for him." I had some money, about a thousand dol-lars, put to one side in case anything went wrong at home. I gave that to him.

"You'll get it back, man," he told me, "with interest and if you want to come up there there'll always be a place for you." It was the last I expected to see of my money.

Bad and all as he was, the band fell to pieces without him. We started arguing among ourselves about what we should play and about who should play solos. We lost our focus. One night, before a gig, I found the drummer and bass player in the toilets of the bar where we were playing. They were cutting white powder into lines with a credit card, the drummer's fingers wrapped like vines around it. "What the hell are you two doing?" I shouted. They offered me some and when I refused, they called me a tight-assed Mick bastard. That was the night the band finally fell to pieces. The two of them played solos through every piece we played, hammering and battering—feedback humming from the speakers—the bass behind me—each chord like a shotgun blast.

Finally it was Caulfield who rescued me. There was a man looking for me, the Sligo barman in the Roaring Twenties told me. Sligo and myself were friendly. A small stocky man with a beard, who didn't trust too many people, he was good enough to let me use him as a forwarding address. "I told him nothing," he said. "He had a northern accent."

Caulfield had come back and straight away had walked into a rent-controlled apartment. "You look like shite," he told me. "Do you ate at all?" The music I was playing was shite as well. I was letting my auld boy down, he told me. "For fuck's sake, it's bad enough when someone useless does it but you have the music at your fingertips. Why did you jack in the job I got you?" I said it was hardly much of a job. "And you can pick and choose?" he said. "You're fuckin' clueless. That's how it works— you get in there and something better will come along. You'll always hear about work when you're working. Jasus, it takes a better man than you to survive not working."

He had a job as a chippie himself and looked like getting into the union—if he could get into a local he was made—and all that came from chancing his arm. He had got a visa. He was working with a Kerry gang in the meantime, second fixing—mostly renovations; skirting and architraves and some stud work. It was all cash-in-hand. The money could be better but the crack was good, he said, and it was work. He would have a word and get me in on it.

Caulfield was right. The work gave me back a sense of purpose. I was staying with him in his apartment. The one thing about Caulfield was he was always ready for a laugh. He was plagued by Jehovah's Witnesses, Mormons and Born Again Christians. The way Caulfield was he'd argue with anyone. "It must be the way I look," he said and of course he decided it was all a conspiracy to drive him from the apartment, which was up for redevelopment. We rearranged the furniture in the living room and he hid in the next room. When the knock came on the door I opened it. I let the two Mormons in, made coffee for them and talked politely with them. No, I wasn't interested in converting. Then one of them said, "We really came here to see the other guy who lives here." "What other guy?" I said. "The other guy, he's Irish too. He was interested in coming down to one of our meetings." I said I lived there alone, that the apartment was new and there had only been one other person there before me. "He was Irish," I told them, "but he committed suicide six months ago. Big fella, with a beard," I told them, describing Caulfield, an oil-tanker of a man. They put down their coffees and left in a hurry.

We played music together on the weekends, for fun and not for a living. Once I was playing for sport it changed my music. It started to come easier to me. I was learning to be a carpenter, but that wasn't coming easy. Flahive, the contractor we were working for, came onto the job one day. "Hide," Caulfield told me. I didn't know enough to get away with it so I dove beneath a kitchen sink unit. "What's he doing down there?" Flahive asked.

"Ach," Caulfield said, "he's just fixing that auld sink." "What is he—a fucking plumber?" Flahive shouted. I got my marching papers.

When Caulfield came home that night he had another start for me. "You just keep plugging away," he said. "That's how I did it. If you get sacked on one job you get the start

somewhere else until you know enough to carry it off." I told him I was leaving. "Where are you going now?" I must have been wittering on about America and wide open spaces because he interrupted my speech. "Alaska!" he shouted. "Fuckin' Alaska—that's not big sky country. Who the fuck do you think you are— John fuckin' Wayne! It's dark up there most of the time and it's cold. It'd freeze the bollocks off you."

No matter what he said I was determined. Kolinsky had sent my money back. The bar was going well. He was a changed man, he told me over the phone. He'd found the American dream. It was every American's God-given right to make money and exploit their fellow man. I had also won a Morrison visa in the lottery. I could go anywhere.

I could even go home, Caulfield told me. I could, I agreed, but not yet. Caulfield didn't like the sound of Kolinsky and he was convinced of my capacity for landing in trouble. Still, there wasn't much he could do about it and he borrowed a car and left me out to the airport. He tried to push money on me. "If you're stuck— phone," he said.

"I'll tell you what," I said, "I'll write and I'll see you at home at the fleadh next summer."

Reels at the End of the World

Kolinsky met me at the air-port. I got the feeling he was glad to see me, though with Kolinsky you could never be sure. "Call me Maguire," he said. "Kolinsky's no name for a man running an establish-ment like the Northern Lights. I'll fill you in on everything as we go. Man, you'll like it up here. The place I got you got all the home comforts. I owe you, man."

"What's the job?"

"Music, man, what else. It's a

Singing in the kitchen. Matty O'Brien sings "The Banks of Claudy" at Molly McMahon's ninety-fifth birthday party in her house at Cappafean, Crusheen.

great place for music—all those long nights," he laughed.

The town he was in throbbed with life. It was like a gold-rush town in one of those old westerns, a service town for men working on the pipeline and in the oilfields. There were few women there, Kolinsky explained, it was all men—men learning to be able to live with nothing other than men. It was a place to make a fast buck and get out quick before it turned you and you ended up like everyone else. Even when the days ended and the work got scarce, some of those men wouldn't leave there. It was the wrong climate but it was easy to imagine the place some years ahead—deserted, sage brush tumbling down the street.

Kolinsky had a problem. The last band couldn't handle it—they just upped and left. "You give these men what they want, none of your fairy music here. Play fast and if a fight breaks out don't stop playing. Play fast and they'll drink fast and everyone's happy." Kolinsky still had a glib comment to make about everything—"The only culture in the Northern Lights grows on the glasses," he said.

That first night I was in a cold sweat before I went out to play. Kolinsky promised me a couple of days to get used to the place, to see how his house band fared, but when they walked out I was pitched in. My heart was vaulting in my chest as I looked out from the small room behind the stage. The bar was just that—a bar to stop the men helping themselves to the drink. Outside it was a wide open space teeming with

Young John Naughton of Kilclaron near Feakle—Young John's father was John, as was his grandfather, thus he is still referred to as Young John. A fine concertina player in the east Clare style. The concertina was more often heard in the west of the county and the east is noted for its fiddle players, like Rochford, Canny and the Hayes's. East Clare music is renowned for its melodious, almost dreamy style of playing, and Young John sits well into this. He has lived in Dublin for some years now.

men, jostling and cat-calling. It was the first time I ever played on my own for money and I had always known what to expect from a crowd before that night.

I played faster than I knew. I could feel the notes zinging about the room, as if they were looking for an exit. I played "The Bucks of Oranmore" three times, all the parts of it. Men capered about in vague approximations of dance; they swung each other in dizzying circles, whirling one another into tables laden with drink. They battered bottles off tables and chairs off the floor in haphazard, demented time with my playing. They yelped and shouted for music they thought I might know. Mostly they shouted for "The Turkey in the Straw." I played "The Mason's Apron" so fast Seán Maguire would have had a headache. I played "The Foxhunter's" and reached the part in the tune where the fox is cornered and the dogs bay—and played it over and over when I realized they liked it, the fiddle sounding more and more like the frenzied dogs, the doomed fox. They joined in, their heads

thrown back—chorusing, howling at the ceiling like animals in pain. One man mounted the bar, kicking like a cossack, sending glasses in all directions. The barman furled him with a skelp of a baseball bat. Another joined me on the out-of-tune piano, plonking along with me and hooting like a train. I still kept playing. Caulfield, if you could see me now, I thought, the sweat in pools in my boots even.

When it was all over I sat on an upturned crate at the back of the tiny stage, toweling sweat off me. Someone was still beating time with a coin on a bottle. The howling and barking continued for a long, long time—the howling and barking and the sound of glass breaking.

When it was all over I went out front and found Kolinsky counting money as his barmen hosed down the floor. In one corner there was a pile of glass and broken furniture. He saw me looking at it.

"With the mark-up I got, man, that don't matter. Have a drink; you earned it. You got 'em all lathered up. Man, if you'd played like that with the band we'd be on the cover of Rolling Stone today."

The deal was six hundred dollars a week and found. "You play till the thaw," Kolinsky said. "Try to run out on me and I'll come after you. You get free beer," he added.

Donie Nolan, Connie McConnell and Johnny O'Leary in Hennessy's pub in Miltown Malbay.

There was nothing to do there but drink. The cinema was an old school hall that ran the same film, whatever was most popular, over and over, for weeks at a time, even when everyone had seen it. As the darkness gathered in around them and the winter wore on, the men's drinking grew relentless. They stared into their glasses as if waiting on something to break within them. Fights grew more frequent. Men accused each other of petty crimes. One man was beaten unconscious because he was a suspected homosexual. Another was stabbed over an incident at work. A third man was shot for disrespecting someone's dog.

But other people came to see me play. "The Foxhunter's" was the most popular tune in town. I had made a bit of a name for myself and I was taking it handy on the drink. I was thinking of Caulfield's advice on a man not working days. I was trying to keep my life in perspective and I had, as he said, the music down to my fingertips. I played all the time. I played fast at night and slowly during the day and, in all the time I was there, it never felt like I played more than a dozen or so tunes.

I started to write home regularly. I was playing a lot of music, I told them. It wasn't always the music I'd have wanted to play but, at

Reels at the
End of
the World

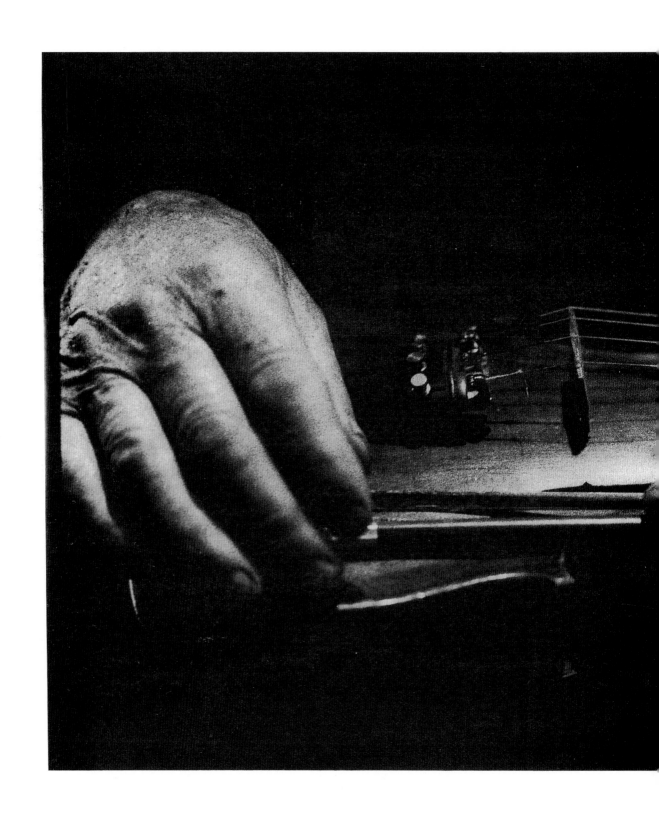

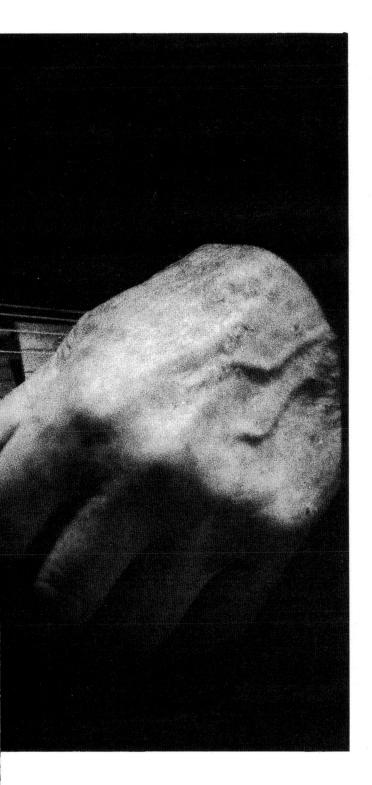

the same time, it was good music. I thought I was learning. I was looking after myself, eating well and all. It was cold there, so cold it was hard to describe, so cold it would be hard for them to imagine; if a carpenter touched the metal on a hammer with his bare hands his fingers would stick to it. I missed them all, I wrote.

That first letter must have eased things for them. They were delighted to hear from me, my mother wrote back. Ann had done well in her Leaving Cert and was going on to be a doctor. They were so proud. Tom was the same as ever, even though he was at university now, studying marine biology; he was after something new every week, one week it was law, the next psychology— you couldn't keep him happy. He was being mentioned for the county hurling team. Mick Talty had died. Just jack-knifed in the kitchen as your father says. They were all back from America for the funeral. The first time they were all together for fifty years. Soon after that

Junior Crehan's hands.

your father's old friend Coleen passed on. He took it bad. He's lonely with everyone away. He goes out of the house at night and stands in that place where he used to stand when he listened to the fox-trots coming across the fields. He never talks about it. What can I do? He won't leave hold of the land. There'll be surprises and changes before we see you again, she wrote. Keep writing. He takes the letter out and reads it all the time. It means a lot to him. It means a lot to him that you stick to the music.

I channeled everything into the music. They sent me out cassettes from home. I listened to "The Bunch of Keys" by Johnny Doran all the time. I would go out walking. It would be like the words of one of those nonsense songs or riddles, going out in the middle of the day, into the dark, into the snow. I would try to remember the way Doran played the tunes. A recorded tune has predetermined endings; every way you could possibly turn is known. I would think of the time I heard an ending on a tune I'd never heard before. "That's not how that finishes," I used to say to my father. "Are you going to argue with Martin Rochford about how a tune finishes?" he'd say. "All you're hearing is variations—as long as it's good 'tis right." That put me in my box. But I could never successfully imagine Doran's playing of "My Love Is in America" or "Rakish Paddy." His music was like

summer weather up there in the dark and cold. It cascaded about me. Agitated like water under the paddle-wheel of an old mill.

I sent a postcard to Caulfield—does this Rooney live or did you invent him? I got one back—he lives. He's beyond in England, in Coventry. You'll get to hear him someday.

I had no music that came from round our way at home yet it was in my head all the time. I was stripping the tunes back to their bare bones. Bleaching them. Imagining them there in that Alaskan snow.

* * *

Between Kilkeshan and The Mills was a great haunt for music. And above in Bodyke and the Blacksticks there is music day and night. Music and the soft cries of water fowl on the lakes and swallows gathering on the wires.

Below on the Burren, scoured from the earth, where God got mixed up and piled the rocks in fields as well as on mountains, where rectangular stones are laid end-on-end in walls, like tombstones resting against a church gable, there is music in all the small towns.

Beyond that to the Cliffs of Moher. Out at sea, between the Hag's Head and Liscannor, lies the drowned village of Kilstephen—those who see it are sure to drown. There is the music of the Russels and Killouherrys, simple music till you try to play it.

Below that again to The Hand and Mount Callan, the "Mist-Covered Mountain." Down again to the Crosses of Annagh and Bonabilla, where the landscape still finds musical form in the compositions of Junior Crehan. Beyond that Spanish Point and the cries of drowned sailors and Spanish soldiers, unable to wade ashore in their heavy body armor.

Beyond that the ocean. Itself the map of an ancient voyage, where the roads exist only in relation to the skies. That way—where the sun goes down—is America, and the other way—where it comes up—is England. That is as much as any man could wish to know.

* * *

I was testing and trying that bit of an air of my father's. But I could never reach it. It was like I had to shake it free of the landscape I was imagining for it. It had to find its own landscape. It was like playing music underwater. Like a dream without narrative, only action and sensation; fish opening and closing their mouths, trying to tell me something. The tunes I stripped bare remained like that—bare. They wouldn't coalesce. They wouldn't dissolve. Each note was separate as a pebble on a sandy beach. I couldn't work them out. I could only collect them.

I tried to let it grow by itself—not to think about it. Then I would imagine music running in vivid colors before me, as I had imagined my father's playing when I lay in bed as a child. I could see myself back in the hollow at Lisnamac, back in the trees. I could still hear music pattering like the first drops of rain off the leaves, the light coming through them and falling on the ground the colors of stained-glass windows. I would grow heartily sick of it all and I would slam the door in the room behind me. I would turn back—open it again and feel the notes quivering in the air. I would imagine them rising like waves of shimmering heat from a furnace. I would close the door.

I told Kolinsky music was a social activity. I yearned for company, for the salt air and cold east wind that Caulfield's driving music brought to me, for the company of a session—for a bad accompanist—for any musician at all—for someone to sing even the odd song. Kolinsky gave me a pay rise and told me that when I was famous I would thank him for keeping my nose at it. I used to play cards with him to pass the time. Silly games where the jack reversed; on seven you picked up seven and a two meant missing a turn; the winner was the one who got out and the loser was left with a fistful he couldn't even hold. When we got fed up of that we'd watch baseball. Kolinsky was a Yankees fan. He had all the gear, the turned-back cap and the jacket. He'd lecture me on their history, on Babe Ruth and Joe DiMaggio, the Yankee Clipper, and

Mickey Mantle who succeeded him. Baseball never meant much to me, but still he'd set up the room to what he called "close as possible to perfect baseball watching conditions." He would ring down to the bar for beer or send someone out for pizza, and he had the lights figured out so he could close his eyes and imagine he was up on the bleachers in some minor-league game as the sun descended beyond the horizon or high up in the stand, in Yankee Stadium, the gloom gathering above the floodlights. For Christmas he bought me a Detroit Tiger's jacket and a book on their history. I was expected to read and learn of the heroics of Al Kaline and the '68 world series team and to be able to argue with him as if I were arguing hurling or football at home or, closer still, the fortunes of some English soccer team. We'd toss a coin and choose one of the teams on the television and, in the end, all the games we watched became largely fictitious affairs where the Yankees were always locked into playing the Tigers.

It was in the seventh inning of one of these interminable games that he first told me about Mrs. Bulfin. "She wants you," he said. "You're to be her protégé." I asked him what the hell he was talking about. "Mrs. Bulfin, old Ma Bulfin, the cultural heart of this here territory. She organizes the classical music concert once a

Turf clamps, County Donegal.

year. Only problem is no one plays classical music up here."

When Mrs. Bulfin came round I was expecting her, but, as Kolinsky suggested, I played it cool and pretended I knew nothing about her. She was a formidable woman, at least as big as Caulfield, and she would brook no refusals. "I believe you're a violinist," she said. I told her I played the fiddle; I wouldn't use the word violin in describing what I did. "No matter," she said. "Do you have any classical music in your repertoire?" I told her that I hadn't. The nearest thing I had were a few Carolan pieces that I had no great time for and might have trouble recalling. I played her a snatch of the "Farewell to Music." She said it would be adequate; "One can't complain up here, although, ideally the concert would comprise classical and light operatic pieces."

I found myself listed in the concert program as playing a minuet by Johann Sebastian Bach. The old schoolhouse was freshly painted for the occasion. Mrs Bulfin had secured, for the first time, sponsorship from the oil company. The money was spent on a professional sound man and lighting crew and, on hearing this, the local radio station wanted to record the occasion for future broadcast.

The town dignitaries gathered in the hall.

the Heartbeat *of* IRISH MUSIC

136

Reels at the
End of
the World

There were so few of them that, from backstage, I could have counted them all gathered in the glow of the footlights. The only face in the crowd I was on speaking terms with was Kolinsky. He sat on his own near the back of the hall. Kolinsky wasn't exactly respectable—he was referred to as the New York drug dealer, even though if that was ever his calling it was in times past.

I was second from the top of the bill, which didn't augur well, seeing that Mrs. Bulfin had never really heard me playing and my piece was less than five minutes long. I came on after a country-and-western singer, a girl I knew from behind the till in the supermarket. I stepped out onto the stage, which was dominated by a grand piano, and played the Carolan, receiving a desultory smattering of applause—apart from Kolinsky and a gang of oilmen who had joined him, who clapped wildly and called for "The Foxhunter's." Then the lights came up and we had an interval before Mrs. Bulfin herself took the stage.

I went back and sat with Kolinsky. He offered me his flask of Wild Turkey. It was cold back there and he was wrapped in a fur coat that he swore came from a grizzly bear; he said he'd traded it for two bottles of whiskey with an old prospector who knew Jack London in the Klondike, way back when. Eventually the lights dimmed again and a spotlight fell center-stage. I could tell from the way the audience released its breath collectively that the night had not gone well out front—they were bored and cold and yearning for release into the snows outside. But, respectable people that they were, they would hold fast and support one of their own; at least Mrs. Bulfin made an effort.

For an instant nothing happened. Then that instant stretched as everybody's eyes focused on the spotlight, center-stage. A few tinkled notes were heard and then they died away. Muffled sounds replaced them, like those of a workman exerting himself, struggling to lift a heavy load.

"Heart attack," a woman screamed. "Someone's having a heart attack," just as the lighting man switched the arc of his beam stage left to reveal Mrs. Bulfin, her shoulder against the grand piano—trying to maneuver it center-stage where the spotlight had first fallen.

The upshot of it all was that it was only myself and the country-and-western singer who were played on the radio. One of their disc jockeys had got hold of the first recording made by the Bothy Band and played it until he'd worn the tape out. He asked me into the studio to talk about Irish music and play live on air. As a result of that I learned how a recording studio worked—how I could layer my playing so that it sounded like there were several people playing, something I knew Johnny Doran had managed to do on an old reel-to-reel recorder, with just the one set of drones, the one bellows and the one chanter.

Then the radio station issued a cassette of music from the oil fields and I became briefly famous on the strength of it. I sent a copy home and one to Caulfield. I wrote back to my father reminding him about the time he had recorded, in London, when a big record company paid five of them to play a selection of tunes as if it was a day's work they were doing. When the engineer detected something wrong with the track he made them play the reels again. And again, and then individually, until he told the box player to stop grunting into the mike. The box player was noted for his expressive style and his exertions were seen as part of that. He unstrapped the box and stood up. "What would you know about it, you Black and Tan bastard?" he shouted. My father wrote back to me for the first time—it was the real thing, the genuine article, he said. I had played "Grogan's Favorite" and "The Sailor on the Rock," "The Longford Collector" and "The Sailor's Bonnet." Maybe, Caulfield wrote, the hard road to the Klondike wasn't such a bad place after all.

The light was back for a long time before I seemed to notice it. I woke up one morning—

my eyes crusted together. The thaw had begun. Beyond the window small patches of muddy brown showed through the snow like mottle on an old person's skin. I had to stamp to warm my feet. My hands felt like they belonged to someone else. I could see the grey rut of the pipeline stretching away in the distance. I could hear the distant whunk, whunk of the drilling rigs.

I went down to the Northern Lights and told Kolinsky I was leaving. He said wait, at least until the world series was over. It was then I had to tell him that I knew we had been watching video tapes of old games—after all, baseball was a summer game, even I knew that. If he was going to end up like that old miner who knew Jack London he would be on his own. I sat at the bar and wrote out a postcard: "Kill the pig. I'm coming home. You'll know me. I'll be the one on the bus with the purple hair." And I signed it C. J. Haughey, the name of the country's leader. I knew that the postman would remark on it and that my mother, who, unlike my father, took an interest in politics and was of the opposite persuasion, would get a laugh from it.

PART FOUR
between the
generations

*Michael Dinan and his brother Tommy.
Tommy is holding the "Russian fiddle."
Tommy was a noted musician in his
younger days before he emigrated to
Birmingham, and he was, reputedly, the
first Clare musician recorded by Raidio
Éireann. He still speaks fondly of the
music of Frank O'Higgins that he first
heard on the radio and of his trip to
audition and then to record in Dublin.
This was in the days before even the
most rudimentary of outside broadcast-
ing units ventured to record musicians
throughout the country.*

The Night Before the Fleadh

Junior Crehan and his wife Cissie.

You could say it was the drink, that it stifled everything within you. You could say it was the work, that it occupied time and gave you no time to think; that way a man would want to die in harness—when he'd brought in the hay maybe, everything rounded off like that. You could say that it was like playing music—if you kept at it you'd never have to think about it, it would just come to you. What-ever you said you were just saying that things would take their course—that you could never do anything about anything. That way it was even more like a tune, it was leading some-where, gathering power, and you would recognize the turn in it coming up. Then it turns out to be a tune that has more than two parts and a choice of endings—like listening to "The Nine Points of Roguery" for the first time, not knowing which way it was going to turn.

The first part of my life was taken up with music, then I married it to my work and crip-pled my hands and got taken up with other concerns. If I'd stayed in Altandown I would have known what my life held. I would have married some woman from within four miles of there. My life would have been tied to the land; it would have had its own cycle—one year much the same as another—taking into account bad weather, bad harvests or just bad luck. But when I stepped on the boat there was no going back—nothing was determined for me anymore and it was chance that I was with Hughie Cailín in Norfolk; chance that I wasn't killed with Coleen Naughton that day, and chance that I met Mary Hynes at all.

When Francie left for America, even though I never said it to Mary, I felt I had failed them all. The house was empty again. My arms had never been a welcoming port for any of them and still I couldn't leave hold of the land. For who or for what, Mary would ask me. In time I couldn't hold onto it anymore, as the stiffness settled deeper into my bones and I couldn't work it. We let some of it out in conacre and Tom began to run the rest. Between studying and hurling and everything else he had a notion to be up to, he kept cattle on it.

I used to go more and more up to Lisnamac, the McMahons', my mother's people's old place, thinking all the while of the great music that had been played and lost forever up there. The whole place was overgrown now with briars, dockins and ancient nettles, their stinging points filled like small white bulbs of pus. I wondered how it could have been forgotten about, that the furze was never ploughed under nor the trees cut for timber. The old pad had disap-

peared back into the grass so that only feet that had been that way many times would know the place was up there and would find their own way, as if by touch, through the canopy of the trees, shaded as a church porch and cool as altar marble, up to the overgrown house—a secret monument to those who left or died at the end of their line. Not a sound up there but for a spring bubbling through the foundations of the tumbled-down ruin.

Then I would go over to the hollow Francie said he heard the music in. I knew every blade of grass in it, but I had never heard anything. When I asked him what the music was like all he could say was "lonely." One of the last stories Mick Talty told me was of my uncle and that hollow and of the music that had driven him to America. I wondered why I was never told that story before. The old man who taught me music must have known it. My mother must have known it. Mick said people just didn't believe in those things anymore, no more than they believed in black dogs or lone bushes—arrah what does it matter, all that's over with now. I didn't hold with piseogs myself, though I took my fire back and I never touched the furze up on the hill behind the house.

I would walk back down into Altandown. Once that summer it rained as I was coming back. It hadn't rained for three weeks. The crops were heavy in the fields and water was in short supply. It was one of those summer rains that starts light and gets heavy, drenching everything. Unless there's shelter near at hand there's no use looking for it—it would be over before you got there. I continued home, watching the fisherman on the lake rowing for the shore, the plash of the oars carried over to me, the waters flustered about the boat, the water fowl cavorting, the bulrushes swaying with the force of the shower. It released the pent-up smells from the earth, the tar on the road was steaming, the ditches dreeping with water and, outside the house, I could smell the geraniums in the window boxes, and the smell of freshly-baked bread, festering in the heat, mixed in with it all.

That night I went to see Tull Dennehy who owned the pub and a fair parcel of land, Lisnamac included. I kept my intentions secret from everyone. What prompted me in the end was that Tull was giving his land over for forestry, planting sitka spruce everywhere. It wasn't the land, I told him, he could keep the land, though if he wanted to sell that I'd name him a fair price. All I was after was the house and the half-acre about it, the half-acre with the trees. Tull was well disposed towards me, but still he was a suspicious man by nature. He didn't get where he was by trusting people, not even his neighbors that he knew all his life. He tried to parley

it into something else. "Trees are the coming thing," he said. "My boy is onto me about getting into the forestry in a bigger way—there's money in them." I said I wouldn't be cutting the trees. "The stone then," he said. "It's back in fashion. Stone goes a good price now and bygod, there's two good caps on them piers up there." No, I told him, I had no buyer for the stone either. It was a family thing; my mother was from up there. I ended up paying over the odds for the old ruin and the trees. But sure what odds, I didn't even know why I wanted it.

After that all I wanted to do was sit at the window. Mick Talty died that November. Mary found him above in the house, dead on the kitchen floor, and they all came back from America and all over. He was so well thought of in death, it was a pity we couldn't think of people in life like that, when it was wanted.

Then Coleen died. His daughter phoned me from London to say they were bringing the body back to Connemara. I drove with Mary up to Galway and was there to help carry the coffin when it came in on the train. It wasn't much of a funeral compared to the sending off Mick Talty got, but I felt it more. No one knew what age Talty was, he'd lived so long. I always felt closer to Coleen than I did to my own brother. Over the years myself and Tom had gone our different ways. Tom died in America and was to be buried

there. We weren't sure where Francie was—only for his friend Caulfield called to the house now and again when he came back we'd have known nothing. There was the horror of lying to your neighbors when they said, "Sure Francie'll be at the funeral." I got a registered letter with an old bankbook for an account in Ennis from America. It was the money for every year the land had been in conacre. He'd never touched it, never spent a penny of it.

At Coleen's funeral there was just us and his immediate family—one brother left alive at home, a handful of cousins, his three daughters—and the priest above in that old graveyard out on Golam Head. I had been up that way once before but hadn't stayed. Someone told me the piper Rowsome was playing in a hotel up in Mayo and I drove on there, dragging Mary with me. I'd only heard Rowsome on the radio before that. It was cold enough out on Golam that day and flurries of snow melted in the air out over the sea that stretched, almost motionless, as far as I could make out. The light was harsh and took some getting used to; it forced your head down towards the rocks that were all the one color with the grey of the sea and the sky, and you would think that that light would never dwindle. I wondered that Coleen never went blind underground—or was it blindness of another sort that drove him there?

I felt useless at funerals—the way you do—wanting to lift a fistful of stony earth from the grave and mold it into something with my hands, breathing on it. Every funeral was part of my own, stumbling beneath my friends.

All I wanted to do now was sit at the window looking out at the empty trees. I didn't want to drink and food had no taste for me. Mary couldn't get through to me. She would all but force me from the house and I'd stand outside, staring down at the geese wintering in the bog on the edge of the lake. I could take no interest in Tom's hurling. I went to a game with him and I saw none of it. I'd have been as well to stay at home and read about it in the paper, and I had to endure people I knew coming up to me and shaking my hand as if I'd arrived back from the dead and they were surprised to see me alive. Mary told Tom it would do me good to get out but it sent me skittering like a rabbit back to its burrow. I couldn't even hear people talking to me. One night I forgot about the couple of cows we kept for ourselves and they made their own way home. After that I used to just hunt them up into the field and leave the gate open behind them.

Christmas morning I was at the window, staring out. We had an old hen that had seen better days; still Mary wouldn't have it put down. I would have had difficulty telling one hen from the other but she knew them individually, good layers and bad. This one should have been in a record book somewhere. To listen to her it was almost human and in its dotage. In its old age it came to believe it could fly, and it would spend its days flapping its wings uselessly. This morning it had somehow risen onto the roof of the chicken coop. It balanced there in the rain, wet and squawking, afraid to get down. I got up from the window to go out and shoo it from its roost and as I did so it fell onto the concrete and lay there with its neck broken.

I took it and buried it where the snow-drops would come up and then I started to cry. I was crying now over stupid things: over a dead hen and how Coleen promised if he died before me he'd come back and give me a knock on the window. He didn't believe in the afterlife. But there came no knock.

Then the music started to come back into me. At first it was like I was lost in a different world, listening to snatches of my mother's tunes that came to me like a language I had no understanding of, carried on the wind and from a great distance. I could hear the chanters, drones and regulators going, the way Doran used to play them; Coleen singing and the water dripping into that hole we were buried in; Mary turning beside me the first night we slept together; the breath between the notes of that

Mayo flute player in the ditch in Lincolnshire; the next thing it would be the rattle of the air gun or the compressor gulping air; or the sound of the train pulling into Euston Station; or the cheer that goes up when the boat docks at Dún Laoghaire. Then it would be Coleman, playing "The Sailor's Bonnet"; the sound of the bellows alone on the accordion; horsehair on catgut; rosin on the bow; the turns in hundreds of tunes.

I took down the fiddle again and it was like a new season, the way you can feel growth in the land for the first time of a year, branches coming where there were only scars on the bark of a tree, nettles showing their heads, briars sending out new suckers. It poured into me like water into a sump hole.

Then I would play with anyone; I would play for a cup of tea and I would play for nothing at all. The first night I went outside the house playing I went down to Dennihey's. I was shivering with fear. Mary was with me, pushing me, goading me to give it a go. Tom Considine's son, Frank, was playing there that night. When he saw me coming in with the case he pulled a chair over for me. Then he went to phone home. There were people in there that night that didn't know I played—the very young, whose families the music was just noise to, but who followed it themselves, for their own reasons, now that it was respectable; and new people who'd moved

The
Night Before
the Fleadh

Martin Rochford from Bodyke in east Clare. Rochford is a noted musician in the east Clare style. Like most musicians from his generation he could never have earned a living from his music; he drove lorries, worked his lime kilns and farmed while rearing his family. But, for Martin, music was always the great passion. He took up the pipes after accidentally hearing Johnny Doran playing, and mastered them as well as the fiddle. Rochford is a man of great wit and humor, who, for some unaccountable reason, appears to have recorded little. But even without recording he has had a great influence on the way in which music is played in recent years, as the sleeve notes on albums from fiddle players like Martin Hayes and Kevin Burke will testify.

into the area—for them I was the man you'd meet on the road who'd hardly talk to you. There was a kind of a silence when I drew out the bow. Considine must have said something to the flute player, who was out for the night from Ennis. "Are you not playing?" I said. "You start, we'll come in then," he said. So I started "Last Night's Fun" and they joined me, flaking into "The Bag of Spuds."

When Francie came home and said to his mother he was going down to Dennihey's for a few tunes, she said, "You'd better ask your father, that's his gig." I was a fixture there.

He started writing long before he came home. He sent a tape and I wrote back to him for the first time. It was great music, I said, but it wasn't just the recording. Plenty of good musicians were never recorded, like the man I learned from. Others were recorded only in bits and pieces that would hardly ever be gathered together. Other recordings, like the one of P. J. Hayes, Paddy Canny and Peter O'Loughlin, you couldn't get anymore. Playing the music was what was important. But it was myself I was telling that to—he already knew it. He was giving his life over to playing music.

When he came back he was a kind of hero, where one time a man who gave his life over to music was a waster. Such a man would have no way of explaining that, maybe, he had no choice

in the matter, music just took hold of you. Then other men would struggle to keep families together, and their lives, like the lives of women who were rarely encouraged to play, were filled with silences, empty spaces.

Not that there were many silences with Francie around. Himself and Caulfield were playing together up and down the country. It was usual for any fiddle player who'd made a bit of a name for themselves to use a guitar for backing; Francie and Caulfield were unusual with the two fiddles; and they tempered each other, Caulfield's vigorous bowing stressing the beat and Francie carrying the melody. They were in great demand.

Old Tull, not being a man to be left out of anything, advertised their last night as an American wake. They'd been asked over to America to play at a festival and would be away for a month, six weeks at most. Neither of them wanted to play by that night but they had to come down this way in any case as they were flying from Shannon. Tull was smart enough to know that they couldn't pull out without accepting part of the blame—the posters were up all over the area and as far away as Galway. It was the night before the fleadh weekend. He had the pub done up and the name changed from Dennihey's to Dennihey's Drink Emporium. I was even on the poster as an added attraction:

THE NIGHT BEFORE THE FLEADH

EAMONN & FRANCIE RUANE

with HUGH CAULFIELD

live in

DENNIHEY'S DRINK EMPORIUM

When we got to the door of the emporium we were refused entrance by a doorman I'd never seen there before. Caulfield shouldered past him. "We're playing music here, you eejit," he said, and inside he wasn't long evicting some poor man from his stool so Mary could have a seat. There was a crowd of Germans in the lounge, playing "The Morning Star," "The Fisherman's Lilt" and "The Drunken Landlady" in the settings they'd lifted from a Bothy Band recording, behind them a bodhrán rattling like calf nuts in a bucket. Frank Considine was driving the music in the bar from one of Cooley's tunes to another: "The Wise Maid," "Last Night's Fun," "The Boys of the Lough" and "Miss Monaghan"—the musicians about him on all sorts of instruments: guitars, bouzoukis, mandolins, banjos, boxes, concertinas, bodhráns, bones and spoons. They'd drift in and out of the séisiún, picking up on the bits of tunes they knew, doing the round and getting lost as he drove into something beyond them. He put down the box and got up to join us and without him the music faltered—all heads were turned to him wondering what to play without him—its

last focus stuttering like a tractor of a frosty morning.

Caulfield was explaining to Tull that he had no intention of paying for any drink and he was going to have his share of it. Around us the crowd heaved and swayed, pushing me left and right. "Let's get this over with," Francie said. They sat down and immediately went from tune to tune in an unending stream of playing. From "The College Groves" and "Toss the Feathers," "The Hunter's Purse" and "The Drunken Tinker" to "McFadden's Handsome Daughter" and "The Girl that Broke My Heart" and both "The Copperplates," numbers one and two. "He didn't get it from the ditches anyway," Mary said to me. A piper sat in, assembled, buckled and launched into "O'Connell's Welcome to Clare," and the music picked up more momentum, the notes from the two fiddles melting in with those from the chanter, the tattoo of a bodhrán, Considine's box punching rhythms through it and a banjo cresting waves of triplets. Outside there were faces pressed up against the window. People were banging on the locked doors to get in. Those inside were calling for tunes, yelping encouragement. You could hear them shouting:

"Give it the bow."

"Skelp it out."

"Play that one you played last night."

"Play 'The Bucks'".

The two of them were like a compression of air in that bar that night.

I played with them when we went back to the house. All our friends came back and people I didn't even know. They took turns at playing music, then the floor in the kitchen was cleared and the dancers rose sparks from the flags. It was the early hours of the morning; most of them had drifted off before I took up the fiddle. I was playing at my own tempo, odd bits of tunes, putting my own endings to them. Caulfield was trying to follow me on my meandering ways and Francie was laughing at him. Finally he gave in. "Jasus," I heard him say, "it's like a dog taking a hare for a rabbit—not knowing its zig-zaggedy ways—he has his own scope, that man."

I could feel the pungent vigor of alcohol dissolving in me and I felt loose again. I handed the Perry fiddle to Caulfield and he held it, admiring the ripple of the grain through it. He contorted his torso in a semi-circle off the chair, sending the notes from the fiddle skimming through the room, bouncing them off the stone flags and the kitchen walls. Then he handed it to Francie.

Notes flurried through the room. Tunes pitched upward, igniting off each other. He improvised, linking bits and pieces of music together with his own joins—parts of tunes, nuances of tunes that were reflections of other tunes. I never heard anyone play with such inventiveness. His face was furrowed with concentration, sweat dripped off him onto the bridge of the fiddle. He seemed four or five notes ahead of the piece he was playing, as if he were waiting on the music to catch up, as if the music were a pure force of his imagination, to be carved from the air by the bow alone. He finished with a flourish, setting and resetting the one tune, suggesting several different endings.

We played for ourselves that night. We played all the tunes we held in common, the music flowing together like liquid from different directions towards the one level. The first white light of morning was breaking over the lake outside before I bowed the first hesitant notes of that air again, expanding it into a slow run. The alcohol tasting sour in my mouth.

"Try this," and Francie added a triplet, and before me, for the first time, that air came together, the notes quivering in the half-light. It was somber music, like waking up to find the blood you'd dreamt of had seeped onto your pillow. I turned it again and again until Francie took up the bow and joined me for the final phrase. I laid down the fiddle and listened to him drag the air out into a hornpipe and slow it into a lament that seemed to settle over the countryside, beyond the open door, like a camphorous mist.

Near Doolin,
County Clare.